Safe, Sexy, & Consensual:

Creating Magic in the Dungeon

Dr. Bob (Robert J. Rubel, PhD)

The Goddess Indigo

Safe, Sexy, & Consensual:

Creating Magic in the Dungeon

Dr. Bob (Robert J. Rubel, PhD)

The Goddess Indigo

Goddess and Doc Press

P.O. Box 171303 Austin, TX 78717

Safe, Sexy, and Consensual:

Creating Magic in the Dungeon.

ISBN: 978-0-9968795-4-5

Library of Congress Control Number: 2020904880

Cover Design: GoddessAndDoc

Layout: Ogunbiyi Ismail

Editor: Patrick Califia

Published by Goddess and Doc Press

Printed in the United States of America

Dedication

We dedicate this book to all the intrepid explorers of the vast universe of alternative sexuality. It can be a strange new world, full of magic, mystery, and mind-blowing good fun. This is also the world in which people often rejuvenate their relationships and connect in ways virtually impossible outside the dungeon. As with all books, what we have written can only be what you make of it. Thank you for allowing us to be a part of your journey. Full speed ahead!

Acknowledgements

We particularly recognize Patrick Califia for his exemplary work editing our book. You certainly have raised it to a much higher level than when you received it.

I, Dr. Bob, also wish to thank Renee St. James for being my Patron for the past many years. It's odd to think of it that way, but that is the reality of it. I simply could not have produced the books that I have without her support.

I, The Goddess wish to express gratitude for my incredible Leather family, my boy, Dr. Bob, and to my dearly departed slave All Ways Yours. They dramatically changed the trajectory of my life. I love and appreciate you!

Thank you.

Foreword

Excellent question!

Dr. Bob and I have been presenting nationally and internationally for more than two decades. Specifically, we have been on the road presenting, facilitating, and conducting three-day intensives about every three weeks throughout each of the years we've been doing this. We have seen and experienced the good, the bad, and the mediocre. We have cherry-picked the best practices from outstanding, well-respected Tops and bottoms, and compiled them here for you. We learn about new techniques continually; we share what we know whenever possible. We realize we don't know it all; there is no "One True Way." We continue to question everything we do in the area of BDSM (bondage and discipline, sadism and masochism) "play." This enables us to give you material that has undergone a lot of scrutiny, personal trial and error, and community feedback.

Dr. Bob and I both began by practicing BDSM and gradually evolved into the M/s (Master/slave) lifestyle. Together, our time adds up to something over fifty years. (It is shocking to see that number in writing.) Actually, I (The Goddess) began in 1986. Slowly and instinctively, I taught my first boyfriend how to serve me. Ultimately, he became my well-trained house slave. In one or another iteration, he remains in my life to this day. As I write this, he's somewhere around my house fixing something.

Most of my long-term relationships involved authority-transfer dynamics; I've always been the leader.

Back then, I did not have the words to describe what I was doing. I found our community and attended my first munch around 1997. I jumped in with my usual thirst for knowledge. Along the way, I became a professional Dominant with an exceptionally successful practice for seven years. I quickly realized that I could not play without establishing some kind of connection with my clients. I had to learn to build rapport and trust rapidly. In those seven years, I was never stood-up by a client. I had some of the highest rates for repeat clients in the industry.

For his part, Dr. Bob stumbled upon the BDSM world when he was 56. However, as a researcher he had, within a few years, devoured the literature about kink, kinkiness, and kinksters. In fact, he has made it his life's mission to understand this culture.

We are both researchers. He has trained for decades to recognize and codify complex theories and concepts. I have spent most of my life refining my ability to apply theory to real-life situations while combining it with empathy and spirituality.

As it turns out, we are well-matched. I instinctively make magic happen. To my honest and continued surprise, he watches me and understands what I do. He sees patterns in my actions and breaks them down into defined, repeatable processes. Who could imagine?!

I am his Master; he is my slave. It is who we are.

WHAT WE KNOW ABOUT YOU, AS OUR READER

Wait. What could we possibly know about you?

Good question!

We've been doing this for a while, and over that time, we have observed some common elements among our workshop attendees and readers.

- Intelligence: Most people who find their way into our community are smarter than the average bear. They have thought about sex beyond preconceived notions of sexual intercourse and discovered this not-exactly-visible subculture.

- ○ Curiosity: The BDSM community attracts curious and creative people. Consider what we think are okay pastimes: fire, electricity, needles... just a guess, but if you took a randomly sampled poll of 50 people walking down any urban street in the US, it is unlikely anyone would think those were usual sex-related activities.

- ○ Connection: In the same way that successful SM scenes depend on "connection," our BDSM community approaches sex, SM scenes, and relationships in ways that would not have occurred to vanilla folks. ("Vanilla" is a non-pejorative term for people whose sexuality does not include BDSM practices or relationship dynamics.)

- ○ Community: We seek friends, teachers, and colleagues with whom we share common interests, usually from within our BDSM community.

So, you are probably smart as a whip, curious, and you want to connect with new kinky friends. You want to be accepted, kinks and all. You want to find others like yourself. This book will help you stand out in the crowd of novices and students who claim to "just be writing a paper." We go beyond the basic mechanics of how to do things: how to throw a flogger, how to do wax play, how to, how to, how to...

In this book, we deconstruct the concept of "BDSM scening" for you. We explain why you do what you do in a scene (a time-limited encounter during which consensual play occurs.)—and how to do it intentionally and reliably to achieve extraordinary results.

By the time you have learned to implement the material in this book, your toys will have become an extension of your will. You will know how to speak a physical (rather than a verbal) language of connection. With practice and application, this will transform your play from the mundane to the transcendent—an experience that goes beyond the limits of a play scene. We will give you a recipe of sorts; a formula for reliably attaining this state.

Are you ready? Here we go!

Contents

"It's still magic, even if you know how it's done." (Terry Pratchett)

"Magic is not a practice. It is a living, breathing web of energy, that (with our permission), can encase our every action." (Dorothy Morrison)

"Take a lover who looks at you like maybe you are magic" (Frida Kahlo)

"Watch carefully the magic that occurs when you give a person just enough comfort to be themselves." (Atticus)

"I do believe in an everyday sort of magic—the inexplicable connectedness we sometimes experience with places, people, works of art and the like; the eerie appropriateness of moments of synchronicity; the whispered voice, the hidden presence, when we think we're alone." (Charles de Lint)

"Magic is not about having a puzzle to solve. It's about creating a moment of awe and astonishment. And that can be a beautiful thing." (David Blaine)

About Magic

What do you know about bringing magic into your life? No, we're not speaking about performing sleight-of-hand or conjuring bunnies from top hats. We're speaking about enhancing aspects of your life that can lift you (and others) out of the humdrum and into something else.

More specifically, we are asking whether you have yet figured out how to bring magic into your play scenes. Let's be honest. Once you have seen a few of them, many play scenes are boring to watch. Often, it's difficult to see a spark of connection between the Top and bottom. The Top is using standard implements in standard ways; no inventiveness, no magic.

Your scenes—and your life—can be more than that. You can learn to create magic in your life and cultivate true connection in your SM scenes. This book is about the latter; learning how to reliably craft captivating, fascinating, magnetic, and connected play scenes with your partner.

But there is a pre-condition. You have to become proficient in each SM play technique you intend to use on someone. By this, we mean that you have become so familiar with your whip or flogger or fire skills, etc. that you can now focus on the overall scene and your connection with your bottom.

Over the course of this book, we will explain how to attain a psychological condition called "flow" or "being in the zone." This state can occur when "expert knowledge is applied under optimal conditions." In the kink scene, it's called "Top-space" and it is often accompanied by its counterpart, "subspace."

Once you are competent in the skills you use with bottoms, we can help you move beyond the well-traveled highways of Rote and Repetition and lead you to the less traveled (yet more picturesque) footpaths of Scintillation and Intimacy. There, you will learn how to stop *trying* to make things magical. You will no longer need to "try," for by that point, you will know how to become one with your scene.

You are responsible for building your expert knowledge. A lot of books have been written about physical techniques and safety. Most local BDSM support groups also offer regular workshops on everything from bondage to clamps to canes and cupping. Soak all of that up; we don't want to duplicate that material here. Our focus is on the emotional, relational, and spiritual aspects of power-exchange.

This book is your guide to scene magic. Come, let's take this journey together. There is a LOT of background to cover before the magic reveals itself.

So…

Welcome!

Let's get started.

Necessary Background

No one is born with high proficiency in a skill. Sure, Mozart was touring Europe by the time he was five. However, few of us are child prodigies. Similarly, we are not born as a skilled Top. We don't instinctively know how to play another person's body like a musical instrument. Becoming highly skilled at something, whether it's sex, music, or astronomy, requires desire, knowledge, and practice. That means "study and application." Anyone can pick up a paddle and swat someone on their rear. It takes experience to know which weight paddle to pick up (and how hard and where to strike) to cause the specific reactions you seek. Once you gain skills in your favorite types of sm play, you will no longer fear hurting your bottom. Now, you will be ready to take them someplace amazing through play.

> Definition: In a sadomasochistic (sm) scene, the person *doing* the action is called a "Top." The word is capitalized to keep you from confusing the word with its usual meaning in English. We aren't referring to the lid of a maple syrup bottle. The person *receiving* the action is called a "bottom." The difference in capitalization also relates to the BDSM culture. In the world of kink, a dominant person is referred to as a "Dominant." Capitalized. While unfortunately confusing, many people assume that "bottom" and "submissive" (or "sub") are synonymous. They aren't.

#################################

This book was sparked by a single paragraph in Guy Baldwin's book, *Ties that Bind*. Guy wrote: "When a body is skillfully stressed physically (through sm techniques) and/or mentally (through power-exchange techniques) you can produce an ecstatic transformation." Wow! That was eye-opening for Bob. In a lightning flash, dozens of little bits of information he had picked up over the years fell into place. This was an "aha" moment. He could now explain how to create "ecstatic transformation."

Bob was working on the class for an event, and it became obvious that this was a book that we could write together. We could add depth and breadth to the material from our unique perspectives. Bob's approach addresses more of the technical and physiological side; my approach (The Goddess) is more psychological and spiritual or energetic.

In this book, we assume you know a few things, such as:

- You know how to handle a flogger (or a whip or your hands or rope, etc.).
- You know dungeon etiquette. For example:
  - You know to become familiar with the rules of the space you are in before playing
  - You know to ask for permission before doing something you aren't sure of (rather than ask for forgiveness after the fact)
  - You know not to play above your skill level
  - You know to keep your voice down around someone else's scene
  - You know not to speak to the players immediately after a scene
  - You know not to touch things that don't belong to you (including people)
  - You know what a dungeon monitor is
  - You know how to clean your tools/toys and dungeon equipment after use
  - You know how important it is to be able to "read" your bottom
  - You know about safety issues associated with all your particular SM skills

This book is about connecting some dots. It is intended to build upon your current BDSM knowledge to help you better understand how to knock the socks off your bottom (if they are wearing any) each and every time you play.

‡‡‡‡‡‡‡‡‡‡‡‡‡‡‡‡‡‡‡‡‡‡‡‡‡‡‡‡‡‡‡‡

Mark Twain said, "It ain't what you don't know that gets you into trouble. What gets you in trouble is what you know for sure that just ain't so." In our Internet-heavy world, saturated with good and bad information about practically everything, it can be a challenge to separate real knowledge from fake information.

The larger, vanilla culture also makes it difficult to separate fact from fiction. Other than studying for our jobs, there isn't much we actually feel required to prepare for. There are many exceedingly important aspects of life our society feels "we just oughta know" either through osmosis or trial and error. Our society seems to tell us we don't have to study how to do such profound things as having relationships, communicating with others, or raising children (to name a few). So we bungle through our relationships, through mediocre communications, and through raising a family, hoping we get it right before it all falls apart.

The world of BDSM is a bit of a paradox. While it's easy to learn physical play skills (flogging, rope, wax play, etc.), it can be much more challenging to discover how to combine those skills to consistently drop your play partner into subspace. Tops are frequently frustrated because they can't figure out why the bottom sometimes goes into subspace and sometimes does not.

Part of the key here is that in the Land of Vanillas, WYSIWYG (What You See Is What You Get). When you see something happening, it usually is what it is; you seldom have to wonder about deeper meanings. This is not quite true in BDSM. In our community, you could walk up on a brutal boot-play scene where someone is apparently getting the @#%$^ kicked out of them. To the untrained eye, this could look like sadistic abuse. However, it may–in fact–be a very mutually arousing, loving scene.

The more you know about this kind of magic, the better able you are to harness it and use it to make memorable play scenes. We believe SM play is equally about technique and intimacy. In our experience, the best scenes combine good technique with a certain amount of magic, spectacle, and trance.

So we wrote this book about magic, spectacle, and trance!

We hope you enjoy it.

PART 1

UNDERSTANDING SM PLAY SCENES

We'll begin with two strong suggestions:

- ALL SM players should maintain current CPR and First Aid certifications. Statistically, the more often you play the more likely your chances of having an "oops." There is also a "learning curve" when you begin any new skill. We all make mistakes; *being prepared* is part of being a responsible play partner. Both the Top and the bottom must be able to assess and appropriately handle safety issues that arise. Responsible, knowledgeable, and well-prepared play partners are sexy!

- *When you arrange a scene with a new partner, have that scene in a public play space. Don't agree to a private scene until you trust this person and feel comfortable with them.* This is true whether you've been in the scene for five weeks or five years. While the idea of getting naked in front of a group of people and playing with someone for the first time might seem daunting, the alternative of playing privately with someone you don't know is risky. And, have no doubt, the risks can be substantial to the Top or the bottom.

Nope. Private play right off the bat is not a good idea. There is no supervision when you're playing privately. There is no one to vouch for this person. There are no witnesses watching should they later claim that the play was non-consensual. You are *not* on a vanilla date; this is *not* just "Netflix and chill."

You may think this doesn't apply to you because you believe you're a good judge of character. That may even be true. However, much like successful con men, successful predators are good actors. And chances are, you've let your guard down a little because you want to play or get played. Desire makes us vulnerable to being less than objective. That opens the door to *risk*.

Speaking of "risk," we would like to point out that when it comes to negotiating a scene with a Top who is new to you, that negotiation must be done with a clear head–and not from a position of submission. The bottom must be able to clearly communicate their requirements, boundaries, and desires from a place of personal power. Think of it as telling the truth rather than pleasing a potential partner. In fact, one of the best things you can find out is how the other person handles not getting their way. Are they mature enough to take the word "no" in their stride, or will they react by trying to manipulate you into softening your boundaries? While many BDSM scenes involve power exchange, it is not appropriate for the bottom to release that power over themselves until everyone clearly understands and agrees to what will and will not be involved in your upcoming scene. Remember that if things go well, you can probably arrange another encounter. You don't have to do everything on your first play date.

The Broad View about sm Scening

Before we get into the trees, we'd like to spend some time speaking about the forest.

sm play has a context. It's an interpersonal sharing and a rather advanced way of connecting with someone.

- First, it's for people who believe there is more to connection and/or sex than fucking.

- Second, it's for "edge-walkers," those who want to push their personal boundaries on their path of self-discovery.

- Third, it's for people who want to have a rollicking good time playing adult games with someone(s).

Perhaps you're a mix of some or all of these. Your answer is the right answer for you. That noted, there are some established rules and protocols involved with BDSM in general and with sm play in particular. This section goes over a few of these conditions.

Advanced dancers will occasionally go back through a beginner's dance class just to be sure their technique is totally correct. This next section is relevant for established BDSM players. It serves as a touchstone. Please take the time to read it so we can all proceed from a common set of assumptions.

A WORD ABOUT SAYING *YES* OR *NO*

For many of life's questions, a simple *yes* or *no* answer is close to useless. For example, your answer to the question, "Would you like to go out to dinner?" hinges on many things.

- Who is asking?
- Is it a special occasion?
- Is it a real question or a rhetorical question?
- What restaurants are being proposed?
- Why not eat at home?
- Do you have the energy and inclination to go out to a restaurant?
- Do you like going to dinner with this person?
- And on and on and on.

As good communicators know, poor questions produce poor answers. It is in the Top's best interest to learn how to ask clear and precise questions when negotiating a play scene. Most Tops know this. However, it is less common for bottoms to realize when a Top *isn't* asking the relevant questions. If the Top isn't asking questions the bottom knows are important, self-preservation (common sense) suggests the bottom must speak up.

Here's the issue from the Top's viewpoint. It is good to know how much *consent* you're getting when negotiating activities that law enforcement officials might consider illegal.

Sloppy, imprecise, or outright misleading negotiations lead fairly quickly down the slippery slope that ends in a consent violation. If you haven't spoken about it, it's off limits. For example, a bottom agreeing only to a flogging has **not** agreed to be touched by your hand unless that was specifically discussed before the scene. A bottom who agrees to a bondage scene does **not** expect to be touched sexually or have any non-negotiated implements used on them.

Remember, when you began negotiating, you and the bottom were probably both dressed. Once the bottom has removed their clothing (if this is a scene where such might occur), they may feel more vulnerable. Also, since they have trusted the Top to the extent of getting undressed, that vulnerability (coupled with initial trust) might cause them to agree to non-negotiated acts. In fact, agreeing to non-negotiated acts when in a compromised state is referred to as *coercion* and/or *intimidation* and has serious legal implications.

Worse (if you can imagine anything worse than this state of affairs), once a bottom enters subspace, they are in an altered mental state. It's not ethical for a Top to deviate from the negotiated activity at any point. Just as you wouldn't ask someone to sign important documents a few hours after surgery, it's not okay for a Top to renegotiate permissions after play begins. There is no clear-cut way to determine when someone is in an impaired state. So don't guess. Stay within negotiated parameters.

If a bottom becomes unsure whether a Top's scene behavior was appropriate, they may begin telling others about it. If, for example, they felt their consent has been violated, the Top could wake up a week later to find their reputation in shambles. Unlike the American justice system where one is considered innocent until proven guilty, a tarnished reputation (with or without real cause) is difficult to overcome. Guilt is often presumed; innocence must often be proven within our community. The Goddess calls this "giving them side-eye." Rumors and disapproval might be the best-case scenario. Lack of trust may lead to the Top being banned or blackballed. In many communities, this can escalate very quickly. You could end up with a criminal record. You could end up in jail.

Be clear: This is treacherous territory with very little room for error. You began the scene giving your word that you would do X. Now you are asking to add Y. Shifting a scene after it has begun is a hard limit for most established SM players. Deviating from the negotiated terms is unethical, regardless how small or seemingly innocent. It can cause you to be seen as a dangerous player. We urge you to remember that your scene negotiations are your promise (your word) that things will go as planned.

The Goddess and I have a lovely friend who for ten years ran an extremely good monthly play party. They were 99% drama-free;

everyone felt safe. After a minor incident a few years ago, she developed a club policy. It was a method for calibrating yes/no answers to measure how *intensely* someone felt about that "yes" or "no." Rose pointed out that by asking a person to rate their "yes" or "no" on a 1–10 scale, you would have a better idea of how emotionally attached they were to their response. "One" meant "Not in your lifetime" and "ten" meant, "This is one of my favorite things."

This calibration system works very well in everyday life and is particularly valuable when negotiating SM play. For example, if the bottom is giving you a *level-8 yes* for flogging, but a *level-9 "yes"* for spanking, you'll know that you're good for both. Similarly, a *level-6 "yes"* reply about their interest in flogging gives you information about how long and intensely you might be able to flog them. It is important to discuss **intensity**, as a flogging with a rabbit skin flogger is dramatically different than with a much heaver, two-handed elk flogger. As you can see, this system helps you structure your scene.

Let me hasten to add that there are some subtleties involved with calibrating in this way. Not all actions carry the same emotional importance. For example, if YOU suggest restaurant X at a *yes-10* level but your partner is only at a *yes- 4* level, whether or not you exert your will and go to that restaurant is largely irrelevant in the long-term. On the other hand, when negotiating a play scene, if you (as a Top) want to do something to your bottom at a *yes-10* level but their interest in having this done to them is anything below a *yes-8*, you had better be *very, very careful about how much of that activity you do and with what intensity.*

Tops: Your honor and integrity depend upon being able to decipher <u>and not exceed</u> your bottom's wishes. While "pushing limits" can seem very sexy and is talked about with bated breath, this is not advisable for casual or pick-up play. If you scare or hurt your bottom, they will feel their boundaries were not respected. This is not the type of reputation you want to cultivate. More importantly, you don't want to damage anyone who trusted you enough to play with you emotionally, physically, or psychologically. It is a much safer choice to play well within the parameters of your bottom's tolerances and your skill level. Leave them happy and wanting a little more; you will soon have a full roster of play dates.

Of course, the opposite situation would be to have few or no people with whom to play This can occur for a number of reasons. Perhaps you don't yet know your craft; perhaps you push boundaries; perhaps (like Dr. Bob) you're socially awkward. On the "pushing boundaries" topic, Tops can unintentionally injure their bottom or get into trouble when they do more than was negotiated, or when they play above their own knowledge and skill level.

On the topic of "social awkwardness," our community tends to be warm and generally accepts people with wide-ranging differences. Please take the time to allow people to get to know you; please take the time to get to know others. In a general sense, you bridge gaps in our community by being dutiful in learning your craft, abiding by safe and ethical customs and practices, and by being of service.

Bottoms, you must be honest when giving your Top a calibrated reply. In our experience, novice bottoms are thrilled by new BDSM sensations. Sometimes bottoms go along with whatever a more-experienced Top has to offer. This is not wise. The attitude that "I'll try anything once" can turn out badly even for the most experienced player. Take the time to understand what you are agreeing to. Make sure you are comfortable. When you take responsibility for communicating with your partner, you enable them to relax and be *in the scene with you*. That is true both for the Top and bottom. Everyone's word has to mean something. Honor and reputation are considered very important in the kink community.

> **Definition: Landmines (Emotional Triggers)**
>
> Words or situations that cause an unexpected (and often emotionally intense) reaction resulting from some prior (and often suppressed) traumatic experience(s).

WHY *PLANNING* IS IMPORTANT

There are two aspects to most scenes: physical and emotional. A physical scene without emotional connection is called a "skills–practice session." An emotional scene without physical skills and/or techniques is called a mess. While we are being a tad tongue-in-cheek, there is some truth to this jest. There are many types of play that might involve creating safe space for an emotional experience where the "skill" or "technique" might escape casual notice (like being a little).

For the sake of this book, we must assume you have some SM play skills. If you do not, it's up to you to find mentors and people with whom to practice your craft to become competent. Skill incompetence leads to hurt bottoms. If we find you are hurting people without consent, we will lock our doors to you. However, if you come to us seeking skill instruction, we will welcome you and offer our help.

There are no shortcuts to achieving excellence in a skill. The Top must practice sufficiently that physical actions become automatic. At that point, they can stop worrying about which toy/tool to use next or how to use it. Now, the Top is able to focus wholly on reading the bottom. This is where finesse begins.

Bottoms will benefit from attending education workshops, receiving some form of mentorship, and playing often enough (with skilled and ethical Tops) to know how to determine that the Top is competent. Once you trust the Top, you can release your conscious mind and enjoy the ride. (You can't get to subspace from tension and distrust.) And let's acknowledge the reality that many BDSM players are switches who enjoy both topping and bottoming, so they will be looking for a high level of competence in both sets of skills.

Now, in the world of business, when a group gets together to accomplish something, they first have to agree what they wish to accomplish. They must define the task and be sure they have the knowledge and skills to solve the challenge. The same is true in kinky play. Before you can figure out how to have a "successful" scene, the two (or more) of you have to understand what you are intending to do, why you want to do it, and whether you have the correct resources (time, equipment, location, etc.).

Are any of you hoping for a long, sensual scene? Does the bottom want a cathartic release? Are they seeking some humiliation play? Do they need to feel they have submitted in some way? Are they just looking some fun at a party? We recommend always asking what all the players need to feel like the scene was a success. Do they need an orgasm, an experience with a new piece of equipment, emotional bonding, or some other type of sensation or activity?

It is crucial to know what the bottom wants. It is also important to know their *whys*. Why did they pick you as a potential Top? Why did they think you would be a good choice for this encounter? You might be surprised by their responses, which reveal the perspective they have of you. This information also gives you the option to bring out aspects of yourself that will complement the kind of scene you're building. (Or the bottom's assumptions may lead you to bow out of the scene entirely.)

For example, if the bottom views the scene as an act of submission, the Top may wish to give the bottom a specific directive to set the tone at the beginning of the scene (once they have completed negotiations). For example, the Top may ask them to get something or do something, even if it's only bringing them a bottle of water. This establishes the Top's authority, as the bottom is immediately engaged in an act of compliance. This goes a long way to setting a submissive bottom's cooperative mental state.

Said even more simply, having a shared understanding helps ensure a successful BDSM experience. The key question: "What is your why?"

- Is this a skills-practice session?
- Is it about having sex?
- Is it about giving or receiving "pleasure?" If yes, what kind of "pleasure?" What does "pleasure" mean to them and you? These questions can also be asked about *"pain."*
- Is the bottom expecting to go into subspace?
- Is the Top providing experiences to the bottom without expecting emotional connection?
- Is the Top (consensually) using the bottom as the Top wishes?
- Is the bottom "proving their submission" by "taking it" from the Top?

"What's the difference?" you may ask. The quick answer is this: Unless you know why you're having the scene, it's hard to orchestrate it. Without planning, what you'll most likely get is a nearly random event that is not particularly special for either of you. Meaning affects what you choose to do, how you do it, and why. It is an important part of negotiation and consent.

Experienced Tops know how to move the bottom from being in a "thinking state" to being in an "emotional state." This skill separates experienced and sensitive Tops from newish Tops. This is a good skill to learn, for it is the key to making the scene a connected experience. We describe ways to create this transition later in this book.

DISCOVERING USEFUL INFORMATION ABOUT YOUR PLAY PARTNER

Topics for a Bottom to Explore with a Top: So, you're a bottom and you've found someone who seems really nice. You want to play with them, but you're still a little new to BDSM play. You're not sure how much you're supposed to know or what you're supposed to do. Well, *knowing that you don't know something* is a good place to be. It's called conscious incompetence. It means you're less likely to get hurt than if you go into this with blind trust or a blustering pretense of expertise.

Some threshold questions might be:

- Who is this person, and why do you want to play with them?

- How long has this Top been in the scene? Some people who have been in the BDSM scene for five years have accumulated a great deal of knowledge. Others have *really* been in the scene for *one year five times*. We are often surprised how little some senior members of our community seem to know. Good Tops seek out continuing education. They never stop learning, any more than good bottoms or switches do.

- Is this Top interested in the same or similar kinks that you are? Said differently, how experienced are they in the types of play **you** are seeking? For example, if you're asking the Top to do X, how do you know that they know much about it? They may have been in the scene a while, but X may not normally be their thing (but they won't tell you for fear of disappointing you—or they don't want to say because they're afraid you'll back out). They also may not tell you because the Top has a big ego and thinks they can do any sm skill you request. Dr. Bob has seen this time and again.

- Are they known for anything particularly positive within the community?

- Do you have friends in common?

- What is their reputation?

- Do you know others who have played with them with the implements you wish that Top will use on you? If so, what feedback will they give you about their scenes?

This is Dr. Bob speaking: I'll share a personal story. I'd been in the scene only about two years. My then-wife and I were on a trip to see my father. Our route enabled us to spend a weekend with a *very, very* senior gay couple we'd met a few months earlier at a weekend BDSM conference in Austin. The Dom was an established author/presenter; we'd struck up a friendship. During this visit to his home, the topic of *flogging* came up. My new friend asked whether I'd ever been flogged. I said that I had not. He offered to flog me. No sooner were the words out of his mouth than his boy immediately said, "You don't know how to flog!" "Oh yes I do," he replied. In retrospect, his boy was right: He didn't know what he was doing.

This was not a great confidence builder. As previously noted, just because a person has been involved with the public BDSM scene for many years and is known to be competent in some forms of sm play doesn't mean that they are competent in *all* forms of sm play.

One time, my friend PhoenixRed pointed out that most Tops have their own specialties. If you're looking for a particular kind of experience, it's good to ask the Top about it. If you're not comfortable approaching the Top directly, ask a DM (Dungeon Monitor) or others (who have played with that person) about the Top's skill in delivering the kind of experience you're seeking. You can simply say, "I want to experience X, can you recommend the right Top?"

This isn't often acknowledged, but novice Tops are often taught their craft by experienced bottoms. It's not beyond the pale for a Top to ask someone knowledgeable about the local community to recommend a bottom who knows their way around a specific type of play.

The bottom line: Not every Top (or bottom) will engage in every form of play. You have to invest some effort to find a suitable partner.

Over our years involved in BDSM, both The Goddess and I have found that our best scenes occurred after consciously matching someone's play wishes with our areas of interest and competence.

Topics for a Top to Explore with a Bottom:

Here are some other questions to consider: who, what, how, and why?

- "Who are they?" In a broad sense, do they identify as a masochist, a sensual bottom, a slave, a submissive, a fetishist, a slut, or...? This is useful information. When starting out in BDSM, it can take time for people to figure out what they want. When you discuss your roles and fantasies before a scene, it can help the Top design the scene around the bottom's chosen identity. You wouldn't play with a spanking bottom the same way you would with someone who likes bloodsports.

- What do they want from the scene? Matched intentions can produce magical results. When your intentions don't match, one or both of you are likely to be disappointed after the play ends.

- How do they resonate with you? Is there chemistry? If there is no chemistry, why do you want to play?

If you are not going to be playing for a few days, consider giving the bottom an assignment of some kind. It doesn't particularly matter what you instruct them to do. You can tell them to dress a certain way for the scene or tell them to physically bring something to the scene (even if it's only a box of tissues). Getting the item requested (or putting the outfit together) creates tangible proof that play is imminent. It's like foreplay.

Also, when the Top asks the bottom to bring something (particularly an odd something), it helps build anticipation, as it arouses curiosity about what is to come. Creative thinking along these lines helps bring excitement—and can be a form of flirting (if appropriate). This also establishes an ongoing connection between the two of you before your scene.

So, you're a Top and you want to play with this bottom. Sounds good. Perhaps the bottom approached you. Still sounds good. However, there can be risks, particularly if you're not very experienced. This is a little different from jumping into bed with someone who turns out to be a disappointing lover. Some of our activities can harm you when misapplied by someone ill-prepared or poorly trained.

Now we're back to questions we brought up a few paragraphs ago: Who is this bottom and why should you play with them? What makes you think they aren't certifiably nuts? Do they come with references? Do you know anyone who can vouch for them?

A note from The Goddess: Gentle (or not so gentle) reader–a word of caution. There are people in our community who flit around the outskirts and either go from friend to friend fairly superficially or go from one demolished relationship to a new and catastrophic relationship almost back-to-back-to-back. These are often the first people to approach novices. We empathize with the desire to forge a quick connection and satisfy fantasies that have been churning and burning your psyche for years. But in the interest of self-preservation, slow down. A really bad time may send you away from the kink community for years. It is worth waiting for a safe, skilled introduction to scening.

Let's put that another way. People who aren't willing to be "seen" or "known" (and people who repeatedly have dysfunctional dynamics) may require an extra hard look before you add them to your play list.

Beyond discovering some basic information about this bottom, what else can you learn? Well, here are a few areas to probe:

- Experience level
- Play preferences
- Medical issues
- Psychological issues
- Limits

- Their relationship with pain
- What they consider *sex* to be, and whether that will be part of the scene

(Tops – ask a lot of questions. You are accountable for designing a safe and successful scene. Someone who doesn't want to answer relevant questions is simply not suitable for play.)

Discovering a Person's Experience Level:

- How long have they been in the *public* BDSM scene (member of a club as opposed to playing on the Internet or privately)? Face-to-face play is very different from hot talk. Make sure they understand the difference as well.

- What good and bad experiences have they had? What have they learned from these experiences?

- What are their most and least favorite toys? Why these?

- Do they prefer *stingy* or *thuddy* sensations?

- Do they prefer to play standing up (Saint Andrew's Cross) or lying down (massage table)? Why? Any physical limitations like arthritis, sciatica, chronic pain, asthma, or other health challenges?

- Does the bottom have their own toys? What kind of toys? Do they prefer the Top to use the bottom's equipment? (Some tools and toys have porous surfaces and can become contaminated with a bottom's body fluids. There can be cross-contamination when that implement is used on a different bottom.)

- What implements or SM experiences do they *want?* This question does not mean you should go outside your comfort zone or skill level to satisfy your bottom's wishes. Being too experimental (especially as a new Top) can set you both up for an awkward and unenjoyable (even dangerous) time. Be careful how far you stretch to please the other person. Tops as well as bottoms have a right to say "no."

- What should the Top expect verbally from the bottom? Do they know how to communicate their safe word (a code word that means "stop," "slow down" or "I need a break") during SM play?

Are they likely to scream? It helps the Top manage the scene when they have some idea of how the bottom communicates what they are experiencing.

O What should the Top expect physically from the bottom? For example, do certain body motions have specific meanings? Are clenched fists different than fingers outstretched? What does it mean if the bottom starts biting their bicep? Will they thrash about? Get sassy or bratty? Squirt?

O Does the bottom become nonverbal when things get intense? If so, how will they communicate during the scene? Some Tops ask the bottom to hold a ball (or other item) that can be released (or made to squeak) if they need to pause or stop the scene.

O What about tears? Does this bottom cry when ecstatic, or when they are unhappy? Do "tears" mean "stop right now," or do they mean "more, please?"

Discovering Play Preferences:

O Are they thinking of role-play, sm play, psychological play, or something else?

O Is the play expected to lead to sex? If yes, how do all parties define "sex?" Is it "sex" if only genital touching is involved? Our definitions of sex are as varied as we are. Take the time to explore this in depth. Also ask any pertinent questions about birth control and prevention of STIs (sexually transmitted infections).

O Is the kind of play that they're interested in also an area that *you are* interested in? That is, will you be stretching your skills, competency, and personal desires in order to play with this person? If so, this may not be a great idea. When you're playing solely for someone else's pleasure, you're not likely to be as attentive (they won't be "all in").

Discovering Medical Issues:

Immediate questions:

- Is there anything about their medical condition that you'll need to know?
- Are they taking any meds that could affect their reactions?
- Do they agree to play without any illegal substances or alcohol in their system? We recommend that negotiation and play be done without mind-altering substances.

Longer-range questions:

- Have they ever had a seizure? Any history of dizzy spells or fainting?
- If you're considering play that would restrict their movements (e.g., rope bondage, plastic-wrap mummification, etc.), do they have any concerns about claustrophobia or knee/back issues? Is there any history of breathing difficulty, panic attacks, or asthma?
- Is there any limit to the amount of time they can play? There are two distinct questions here. First, is there a limit to the amount of time they are willing and available to play with you; second, is there a limit to the amount of time they think they are able (physically, emotionally, etc.) to participate in the planned scene.
- What (if any) accommodations might be necessary before, during, and after play?

PhoenixRed adds: "If they reveal a medical condition, you have to ask if they carry relevant emergency meds. If so, the Top must tell the bottom to instruct them how and when to use the medications. Conditions like arrhythmia, heart conditions, and asthma usually have emergency rescue medicines associated with them."

Discovering Psychological Issues:

You'll also want to ask about their emotional/psychological history. Find out whether they've had any particularly good or bad scenes. If a prior scene went awry, what happened and how can it be avoided in the future? If a previous scene was particularly good, what made it so, and should some of those successful elements be included in the upcoming scene?

Ask whether they are aware of any activities that might trigger them in some way. For example, one person may let you slap their chest and genitals and back and ass—but not their face. Another may let you slap their face and genitalia and punch them in the stomach but warns that if you stick your finger or tongue in their belly button, you'll never touch them again. Intimate questions can be awkward to ask. However, safe play depends (among other things) on the Top knowing about possible triggers and landmines. Tops also have triggers and individual erotic do's and don't's. These are also important to specify.

Discovering their Relationship with Pain:

As long as you're discussing intimate topics, you might ask about their relationship with *pain*—physical pain, emotional pain, or spiritual pain. It might seem an odd question, but it can elicit good information. What sensations (pain, surprise, mindfuck, etc.) will create the type of intensity you want? Unpacking the bottom's definition of "good" and "bad" pain and their relationship with pain will help you determine how intense you are able to make the scene.

Pain comes in two general categories: "good pain" and "bad pain." When the Top provides good pain, the bottom will ask to play again. When the Top provides bad pain, there may very well be consequences that extend beyond their personal relationship.

Here are some other questions related to pain.

- Are they masochistic, or are they "taking the pain" as their role in the play, or are they mostly curious about the sensations? Put another way, are they a masochist who seeks pain because it is a turn-on, or are they a submissive that will endure pain to prove that they belong to or are suffering for the Top?
- Do they seek humiliation, and if so, why?
- Are they playing for *their* pleasure or *your* pleasure?

- What do they hope to get out of this experience?

- Are any *words* off limits (e.g., bitch, pansy, cum-bucket, bastard, cunt, slut, whore, etc.)? In all honesty, it is better not to venture into name-calling with someone until you know they desire it. This can take very specific negotiations. Two words that look like synonyms to the Top can have quite a different emotional valence for the bottom.

- How do they define after-care, and how should it take place? Would they like to be left alone after the scene (and after-care has been administered) or would they rather you contact them the next day for a check-in?

- Do they want after-care at all? There are bottoms (and Tops) who don't do after-care and attempting to do after-care could counter the effects of a good play scene for them.

(By the way, if you are interested in exploring the concept of *pain,* we recommend the book *Sacred Pain: Hurting the Body for the Sake of the Soul* by Ariel Glucklich (Oxford, England: Oxford University Press, 2001. Print.). This book examines sacred pain and observes that ritual pain can be transformational. He draws on the fields of psychology, neurophysiology and religious studies.)

Discovering Their Limits:

That last bullet brings us to the topic of *limits.* There are a number of kinds of limits. Some of those appear below. While negotiating, think about:

- Limits on the types of *activities* they wish to experience (perhaps no scat or blood play);

- Limits on the use of *psychological torment* (perhaps no verbal violation or humiliation play);

- Limits to the scene's overall intensity (do they want *cathartic release*—crying, etc.); and

- Limits imposed on marking them. Some people treasure bruises left after play and others cannot be marked.

Discovering Whether Sex will be Part of the Scene:

As mentioned before (and it's worth mentioning again), some tricky issues come up when discussing sex play. For starters, adults are split when it comes to naming what "sex" is. For some, they're having sex if any erogenous zone is being touched; others only call it "sex" when there is penetration. Some consider sex to be certain types of intimacy that may not involve genitals at all.

This brings us to the point of negotiating "sex" during play. First know that sex doesn't have to be a part of any scene. If both parties desire sex, then you will need very clear and concise negotiations.

What body parts are off limits (e.g., breasts, chest, genitals, feet, underarms, etc.)? How about fingering? Are there any types (or sizes) of toys that are specifically *not* to be used? If you intend on engaging in sexual acts, are you following safer sex practices? Do you agree on what those practices are? For example, once bodily fluids are involved, every toy/tool touched by that Top is now contaminated. So are their fingers and, perhaps, parts of their body and face. A related question: How were toy/tool surfaces and handles cleaned before this play session? Did you use a product that will kill viruses? Take the time to unpack what "safer sex practices" means in no uncertain terms. We all have heard the adage about what happens when we assume, it makes an ASS of U and ME.

Dr. Bob knows of a recent case where improperly cleaned vibrators used on one female play partner transmitted a very serious case of HPV (human papillomavirus or genital warts) to a second female play partner even though the play was days apart. The heads of the vibrators had been encased with condoms, but the handles were probably contaminated. HPV is very easily transmitted, on toys or fingers or genitals, so being scrupulous about cleaning toys and using viral barriers is mandatory.

Hint: Many seasoned Tops wear two (or more) sets of protective gloves for "messy scenes." Once a glove is contaminated, it can be discarded quickly so the flow of play may continue uninterrupted.

While most negotiations go swimmingly, some don't. Sometimes, the Top or bottom is withholding key information *or skewing their answers because they think that's what the other person wants to hear.* This is a time to rely on your negotiation protocols and also your gut reactions to their responses. Did you feel everyone was being honest? Were they consistent? Did you feel respected and heard? Did you feel the questions and answers were made with integrity? Did your potential partner have references? Are they known within the community?

By this point, you probably have a decent idea of who you are playing with and are confident the scene will be mutually enjoyable.

Bottom line: You're now off to a great start.

INTRODUCING THE D/S (PSYCHOLOGICAL) DYNAMIC

Up to this point, we've been using the terms *Top* and *bottom* more often than *Dom* and *sub* when describing two people participating in a scene. We have been careful to do this, as the words "Top" and "bottom" roughly explain who is "doing" and who is 'receiving" the action. We are now clarifying these two words with extreme caution.

These words have caused agony in our community since the first person consensually knelt before another. When we hear "dominance" and "submission," a whole slew of stereotypes and biases are sure to emerge. We aren't using these words as boxes to confine you; being "dominant" or "submissive" should look just the way you want it to look. On the other hand, words such as "Dominant" or "submissive" can be used to broadly describe personality traits that involve *psychological* dimensions that affect scene dynamics.

Master Skip Chasey and Master Steve Sampson phrased it this way: "Top and bottom are about the physical body; Dominant and submissive are about the mental body."

While virtually all kinds of scenes seek to build connection between players, Top/bottom scenes are different than D/s scenes. D/s scenes often involve "power exchange." That power exchange can color the interaction with different psychological (and sometimes spiritual) components.

It is important to clarify whether you are in a *power exchange scene* (where one of you is clearly the Dominant and the other is clearly the submissive), or a *sensation-only scene* between a Top and bottom.

Unlike a Top/bottom scene (where you can pretty much say: "Okay, bottom, the spanking bench we negotiated is open. Let's go!"), a power exchange D/s scene requires different staging and subtlety.

How you start something is often how you end it. As the Top, your pre-scene task is to establish the bottom's mental and emotional states. The success of your scene depends (to a large extent) on your success at this point. Overall success or failure can be tangible: Did the Top and bottom have a transcendent (extra special) experience or was it rather like another day at the office where nothing very interesting happened? Asked differently, was the flogging just a flogging, or was it an OMG! HOW DID A FLOGGING BECOME SO MAGICAL? If it wasn't a WOW experience, you definitely have room for improvement.

> You only have one opportunity to get this scene started down the path you are seeking. *What you say and do—and how you say and do it during the scene's opening moments is, itself, an art form. "Starting a scene" should be its own magical moment.*

Through words and actions, the Top must learn to do four or five things at the outset:

- Create and maintain connection with their bottom.
- Take control of the bottom (if it is a D/s scene),
- Communicate pertinent safety information.
- Align scene expectation.
- Establish and maintain control of the scene.

Tops must develop their own styles, to be sure. However, what you say, how you say it, and how you interact with the bottom combine to demonstrate your sensitivity to them. In fact, the way you handle your bottom also demonstrates both your *leadership* competency and your own personal *flair*. Also, you may want to research a bit about the psychology of leadership and dominance. You're not in Kansas, anymore, Dorothy.

PROTECT AGAINST BEING HURT OR HURTING ANOTHER

The last thing anyone wants is a scene-ending safety issue. Certain steps reduce your risk.

It is crucial to vet anyone with whom you are going to play. In our community, it is *absolutely appropriate* to ask others about a potential play partner's background, history, reputation, and play style. If you are both in the local community, ask around. If you are at a distance, inquire with the leaders of groups in which your potential play partner is involved. It is a strong "red flag" when someone has *few or no* ties within their community.

Take the time to look this person up on Fetlife and other social media. Do they have many friends? Are they in relationships? Do they belong to any groups? If you have friends in common, contact a few. Such research can help you start forming an idea about their character, skill level, and reputation.

We strongly recommend against playing with someone who can't be vetted. It's really unsafe. Playing with someone new, no matter how exhilarating isn't worth the potential cost (e.g., death, abuse, legal consequences, maligned reputation, etc).

After you are confident you have selected the right Top for the scene, you are ready to negotiate the details. Unless you are an experienced negotiator, we strongly recommend having a "negotiation buddy" to help you. Your ideal negotiation buddy would be someone who has been in the scene for some years and can look out for your best interests. This negotiation buddy might help you prepare for a conversation about play. They may be present while the scene is taking place. To gather feedback, you may want to check in with them after negotiation and again after play.

While introductory SM play (such as light sensation play or sensual toys) is pretty intuitive and can be carried out without knowing much about style or technique, many forms of SM play can be dangerous and should be learned from a hands-on mentor. The human body is a beautiful instrument that can be played in amazing ways. However, as with all skills, improvement requires practice. Moreover, you will become more skillful as you better master your instrument ("instrument" = the human body in general, and your chosen bottom in particular).

Since this isn't a book about *how to do* SM play, we're not going to spend much time giving safety warnings, but we will mention a few so you get the idea. We strongly encourage you to learn (and hone) your craft. Frankly, it's your personal responsibility to take the time to learn about the techniques you wish to use and also to learn something about the human body. Successful play scenes result from Tops who have developed competent SM skills and have mastered basic knowledge of human anatomy. Bottoms who also have this knowledge are better able to assess Tops and communicate their own needs.

Our first and most strident safety advice for bottoms is that they learn how to do what they want done to them. As a bottom, you have a personal responsibility to know safety standards for each type of play. You can't know if the Top is being responsible unless you know what "responsible" means. You may have heard the Russian expression: "Trust but verify." It applies here as much as it would to inspecting nuclear research facilities. Bottoms might trust their Tops, but also need a way to verify that trustworthiness.

That said, here are some examples of **pre-scene** discussion topics:

- Is the Top's skill level appropriate for the activity being discussed?
- Can the bottom be trusted to communicate their level of distress (such as calling "red" or "yellow")?
- Do either of you have mind-altering drugs or other intoxicants in your bodies?
- Is there anything unusual going on that needs to be discussed? (Sleepy? Body ache? Bad mood? Bad day? Hungry? Hormonal issues?)

Here are a (very) few **safety** concerns you will probably want to discuss.

- Are you both certified and current in your First Aid and CPR?
- Where is the First Aid Kit and what is in it? Does it hold the usual items you might need in case of an "oops?"

- Bondage in general: Bottoms… only allow yourself to be tied by someone you trust. Also, be sure the Top has the correct equipment to quickly cut you out of or unlock any kind of bondage scene (rope, plastic-wrap, duct tape, chains, etc.). Typically, that means the Top has EMT medical shears and keys within reach, but if you're doing a handcuff scene, it would mean you would have the handcuff key within easy reach AND a backup key somewhere else in the same room. If the scene involves chains, then the Top would have a bolt cutter large enough to sever either the chain or the lock. Tops: You might wish to instruct the bottom to call out a body part (as opposed to a safety color such as "red") where a knot or rope-*Twist* is uncomfortable.

- Suspension bondage: Top: Insist your bottom do stretching exercises before the scene. Are you using OSHA-rated quick-release devices between the overhead anchor and the bottom's cuffs? Make sure your equipment is rated to safely handle the weight of your subject.

- Cuffed hands over the head: Often, blood flow is restricted when someone is tied up with their hands overhead. There are standards for checking skin temperature and color. Does the Top know these? Also, as mentioned just above, BDSM "best practices" use an OSHA-rated "panic snap quick-release" connector between the anchored eyebolt and overhead cuffs so the suspended person can be quickly brought down by one person (should they faint, for example). Does the Top know that handcuffs are inappropriate for suspension? Do they have the right kind of cuffs to protect nerves, joints, and muscles from damage?

- It is *extremely* important to know these things. I (The Goddess Indigo) once had a bottom who neglected to mention that they usually passed out when their hands were over their head. I placed him on a St. Andrews cross and snapped his ankle restraints and then raised his wrists and placed them in the upper restraints. As soon as I was placed the last clip, he became dead weight. That was a terrifying experience. I had safety precautions already in place, but it could have gone horribly awry. As a woman playing with a man, physics were against me. Being able to physically lift a man's dead weight with one hand while trying to unclip them from some device with the other is nearly impossible. You MUST use panic-release snaps. They solve this issue because they can be released instantly with only one hand with the full weight of an unconscious person dangling below. (By the way, for those who are technically minded, snap-release connectors are sold based on the amount of weight they can withstand before breaking. The kind of snap-release connectors sold in tack shops is quite different from those sold for mountain rescue teams.)

- Fire play: A bottom should *never* be tied to anything during fire play. Every single fire play disaster I (Dr. Bob who specializes in fire play) ever heard of involved a bottom who was tied to something. Make no exceptions to this rule.

- Gagged bottom: How will a gagged bottom signal "yellow" or "red?" Perhaps have them drop a bell or ball. Make sure your chosen system will work in a dark, crowded, loud dungeon. Furthermore, some people dislike keeping their mouths stretched opened for a long time; it hurts. You demonstrate thoughtfulness and care (and build the bottom's confidence in you) by verifying in advance that they can perform the activities you're intending.

- Stopping the scene: Either a Top or a bottom has not only the right but the obligation to stop a scene at any time for any reason. Perhaps the scene isn't going as they wish; perhaps they are tired, have had enough, or are just not having fun. The Goddess and I have both seen cases where the Top became uncomfortable with the lack of feedback from the bottom and stopped their scene rather than risk being accused of a consent violation. Both The Goddess and I have ample experience where a bottom called halt to a scene. In one case, the music wasn't right; in another, the scene started too intensely; another time the room was too cold. There are all kinds of examples, and all of them are valid.

While you are scening, the Top must never leave the bottom by themselves. It doesn't matter where you are playing—a public dungeon, your own bedroom, or a private party. Shit happens when you least expect it. You don't want to have to explain to the police why you left a bottom restrained, gagged, and alone while you ran out to get some Rocky Road ice cream.

Don't get drunk or high if you are playing by yourself. "What? Playing alone? As in, nobody else there? Why can't I drink or smoke and do some SM play if I'm alone?" Answer: Because in an altered state, you might think that something is a really excellent idea when it's actually little more than an opportunity to win a Darwin Award.

Have you ever scanned the stories about those who have won Darwin Awards? They are about people who have removed themselves from the human gene pool because their "good ideas" weren't so hot. These stories make interesting reading, and we urge you to look at a few of them before you think about playing alone while using mind-altering substances.

At any rate, if you're playing solo, be sure you can still reach your cell phone. Of course, a fully charged cell phone within your reach isn't very helpful if you are experimenting with autoerotic asphyxiation. That leads to an easy work-around: Fill out a Darwin Award application *before* you begin to play with autoerotic asphyxiation. As a side-benefit, it saves the police some time trying to figure out why in the world you did this.

Note: We both know people who do autoerotic asphyxiation. We are not trying to kink-shame. As seasoned players and international presenters, we cannot endorse this form of play under any circumstances. As Jay Wiseman likes to say, "Avoid kink play where an 'oops' can result in death."

But you know all this, right? And you also know better than to play with relative strangers.

Here is a true cautionary tale. If you want to know how NOT to start in the BDSM scene, read on.

> Recently divorced and looking good, you have gone to an upscale hotel for a vanilla "singles meet-and-greet." There, you discover a tall, dark, and handsome man with an exotic accent.

(Remember: true story.) You've got a *thing* for gorgeous men with exotic accents. He's a brilliant conversationalist, smooth as glass, and you really like him. You like his body; he likes your body. He says he lives nearby, and if you would like, he would be glad to take you over to his place for (uh-hum) drinks…

To his surprise, you tell him that this sounds like a great idea! He offers to drive you to his home (although he realizes you've clearly driven to this social event and he will now have to bring you back to your car). You accept, deciding that he looks and sounds safe—so you don't bother to go back to your car for your cell phone. You proceed to his house where he graciously offers you a drink and begins to show you his BDSM toys.

Well, now. This is an eye-opener. You have never even *seen* BDSM toys up-close. He shows you his spanking bench and Saint Andrew's Cross—like props from scary movies; you are titillated. After about an hour, he calls you a natural submissive and you ask him to explain that word. After a little more wine and talk, he asks you if you want to be his slave. Your head is reeling. BDSM? What's a submissive? Slave? You're a nurse— how do you get from RN to *slave*?

Ultimately, he takes you back to his car. You sit there in the dark with your heart racing, reliving every torrid moment. Suddenly, you realize… "Wait, he didn't even try to fuck me! Like: What the Hell???"

This was how the woman who later became Dr. Bob's slave (for eight years) first discovered that there even WAS a BDSM scene out there. Home from this date, she looked up *submissive* and proceeded to find a local BDSM club meeting she could attend. Dr. Bob happened to be the door monitor when she walked into her very first-ever BDSM event. She sat next to him and he tried to explain what she was hearing during that meeting. The presenter, a very senior Leatherman visiting from the East Coast and presenting on an advanced topic, might as well have been speaking Latin.

She was extraordinarily lucky. The man who picked her up and took her home was well-known and well-respected within our local kink community. He is a fine gentleman with unquestioned integrity. Dr. Bob had met him a number of times and liked him. This story could easily have become tragic. Don't depend on luck. Don't go home with strangers.

ENDORPHINS FROM ADRENALINE

Note: Much of the negotiating we're about to describe has to do with whether or not the scene is going to be an adrenaline/endorphin event or something else.

You will hear a lot about "Top-space" and "subspace." These emotional states result from your brain flooding your body with some mix of adrenaline and endorphins. In a scene, certain activities can produce these chemicals. It will help you orchestrate your scenes if you understand how to manage endorphin or adrenaline release in your partner (and yourself).

Adrenaline is usually triggered by excitement, stress, threats, or fear. It activates our "fight or flight" reaction. Operated by your amygdala, it adds oxygen into your system, sharpens your senses, and can decrease your sensitivity to pain. You will notice an increase in heart rate and blood pressure. Effects can last up to an hour.

Endorphins cause your heart rate and blood pressure to decrease. While adrenaline is produced in the adrenal glands, endorphins are produced primarily from the pituitary and hypothalamus glands. These chemicals have powerful natural pain-control capabilities. You must be able to judge when your bottom is so flooded with endorphins that their ability to assess pain is distorted. This means you have to know when to stop, even if your bottom doesn't.

Avoiding an "Oops:" Negotiations and Negotiating

Much in life involves conversations that really are negotiations. You may not think of them as negotiations, but they are. Just the simple phrase, "What's for dinner?" can open the door for negotiation and compromise. You may negotiate with your boss about work assignments.

Although the word *negotiation* sounds formal, it just means discussing something and figuring out how you and others are going to resolve it. In the case of SM play, the Top is offering certain skills and both Top and bottom are explaining what they hope to experience, and what is okay and not okay during their scene.

Honestly, your scene starts when you begin discussing play options. That's the time to start building excitement and anticipation. Depending upon the situation, this can go on for days or only for minutes. Once you realize that "scene negotiation" is a form of foreplay, chances are your negotiations will take longer and be more fun. Done right, it is a time to be flirtatious and creative. It's a time for each of you to dream of the event and think up creative ways to play together.

The Top might want to hear all the naughty little details of the bottom's fantasies. They may want to know what the bottom is afraid of as much as what they desperately want. They may want to know what turns them on or off, and what they are willing to do (or experience) to get what (or where) they want.

Unless pre-negotiated, do not do this sort of flirtatious banter during the scene.

NEGOTIATION AS A CONCEPT

The word "negotiate" has multiple meanings. In one sense, it means "to find a way over or through (such as an obstacle or a difficult path)." This idea permeates how we look at scene negotiations. Many people look at *negotiation* as a chore. They see it as a kind of tedious but necessary exchange they must go through to get to the really fun things, like play.

We submit to you that scene negotiation is yummy stuff. This is when you get to pull all the ingredients together that will make scene magic. You establish your connection, trust, and yes, limits. Within the confines of the recipe you both construct, you are able to concoct a true masterpiece. Take the time to relish the negotiation process. Find joy in the details. They will stand you in good stead as you create magic together.

A mild warning: Knowing someone socially may not help you when it comes time to create a scene together. "Why?" you ask. Because you may take liberties you would not take with someone you don't know socially. Your familiarity may lead to unwanted or intrusive intimacies. In fact, when playing with a social friend, you may have abbreviated the scene negotiation process.

This section is meant to clarify and stabilize the negotiation process and help keep you out of ethical trouble during your scene.

A word of caution: "Customizing your scene negotiation" is really a case of "skipping steps based upon your perceived familiarity." It is a slippery slope. An airline pilot doesn't skip steps on their take-off checklist simply because they are familiar with the plane or because it's a perfectly sunny day. The negotiation process is there for a reason, and stories about those who gloss over these steps often become our scary examples in books and workshops.

We feel strongly that having a defined and repeatable process will increase your chances for successful scenes. Much like the airline pilot, rigorously following the "pre-flight checklist" increases the likelihood the plane (scene) will reach its destination.

Scenes succeed or fail to the extent the scene participants (whether two or 20) have aligned expectations. You get to aligned expectations by discussing the proposed scene. As you have been reading, this is called negotiation in our BDSM world. Fundamentally, this is the time to find out what each of you seeks from this experience. What do you expect to feel or experience during and after play? Are you expecting repeated play from this person? How long do you intend to play, how intensely, and so forth?

Beyond knowing about the bottom's physical and mental health and level of sm play experience, it helps the Top to know what the bottom hopes to get from this experience. For example, the bottom may want:

- To experience new kinds of sensations.
- To go into subspace.
- To have their limits pushed.
- To serve as a demo bottom in an educational setting.
- To explore fantasies they've had for years.
- To feel your touch.
- To become a long-term play partner, or
- To have a close bonding experience with this Top.

There's another important match to make: Where do each of you fall on the "masochist-sadist" scale and the "service Top-sensualist scale?" This plays out in the kind of scene the Top designs. For example, in one case the Top might plan a scene where the intensity builds and builds, but in another case, they might supply a variety of sensations, none of which are very intense at all.

How Much I Like:										
Stingy	1	2	3	4	5	6	7	8	9	10

Intensity Scale:										
Stingy	1	2	3	4	5	6	7	8	9	10

How Much I Like:										
Thuddy	1	2	3	4	5	6	7	8	9	10

Intensity Scale:										
Thuddy	1	2	3	4	5	6	7	8	9	10

Sensual	1	2	3	4	5	6	7	8	9	Sadistic
	1	2	3	4	5	6	7	8	9	10
	1	2	3	4	5	6	7	8	9	10

> Note: While a masochist derives erotic stimulation from what most of us would call "pain," a *sensationist* enjoys experiencing a range of feelings produced during SM play but does not do well with pain.

Ultimately, the goal is to ensure that each person's *wants* are met without violating either person's *needs* (not to be traumatized or harmed physically, mentally, etc.).

If you expect your scene to be successful, your negotiations have to be successful. This is the kinky version of a basic business model: "Successful project execution depends on successful business planning."

> If you expect your scene to be successful,
>
> your negotiations have to be successful.

THE MECHANICS OF NEGOTIATION

The negotiating process is extremely important as you engage in this lifestyle. Reputations rise and fall based on the bottom's reactions to the Top's behavior before, during, and after a scene. Trustworthy Tops can stand up to the most stringent ting processes; untrustworthy Tops become embroiled with drama and are frequently moved to the outside of the kink circle. Untrustworthy Tops will have trouble finding bottoms who will play with them. The same is true of bottoms who do not negotiate in good faith.

Clear communication increases your chances of success. This is true in all aspects of life. In SM situations, poor communication frequently leads to trust and consent violations. In extreme cases (for example, where multiple bottoms report consent violations by a particular Top – or *vice versa*), that person can find themself banned from parties or clubs.

(Note: While not common in all locales, we know a community that has an organization comprised of officers from most local BDSM clubs. They receive reports of consent violations. They start a file on that person/situation and make that information accessible to all group leaders who are part of this organization.)

So...

Please learn how to negotiate. These discussions about negotiations are as relevant for established BDSMers as they are for those still fairly new to the scene.

Once you have participated in BDSM clubs and parties for a few years (and watched others Top and bottom), your negotiations are more likely to sound like this:

≠≠≠≠≠≠≠≠≠≠≠≠≠≠≠≠≠≠≠≠≠≠≠≠≠≠≠≠≠≠≠≠≠

Top: "You wish a medium-strength impact scene with me, correct?"

Bottom: "Absolutely, that would be great."

Top: "I would like to use canes, floggers, and my hands for this impact play scene. Are all of those implements okay?"

Bottom: "Yes, they are all fine."

Top: "I will cane your buttocks and thighs as well as flog your buttocks, stomach, chest, and thighs. No touch or implements on your genitals, correct?"

Bottom: "Yes, that is all great and thank you for avoiding my genitals at this time."

Top: "Fantastic, I'm in. Now, let's discuss how we are defining 'red' and 'yellow.' Just to make sure we are on the same page, please tell me what 'yellow' and 'red' mean to you during a scene."

Bottom: "Well, I'd say 'yellow' means 'slow down and let me process,' 'red' means stop."

Top: "Perfect, I use those words the same way. Our scene sounds wonderful. Is there anything I need to avoid—health concerns or physical limitations? Do you have any strong preferences that we've not already covered?"

Bottom: "Actually, yes, thanks for asking. I'm a bit claustrophobic, so I'd prefer that you not restrain me. I can only stand for about 30 minutes at a time. Also, I don't need much warm-up, but I would suggest watching my hands for my reactions. If all my fingers are stiff and pointed out, I'm processing the intense sensations. If my fist is clenched, I'm on the ride. As I said, I'll call 'yellow,' if I need more processing time."

Top: "Then we will use a spanking bench rather than a St. Andrew's Cross. I understand all that. Any landmines or triggers I need to know about?"

Bottom: "Yes: please don't put your hands around my neck—it feels creepy. And don't tickle me. And, although we didn't discuss it earlier, please don't cane or flog my feet."

Top: "No hands around the neck, no tickling, and definitely won't mess with your feet. Can you speak during play?"

Bottom: "Sometimes I become non-verbal but will stomp my foot if I need you to check in with me."

Top; "So, stomping your foot is a yellow and means to check in on you?"

Bottom: "Yes, please."

Top: "Good signal. Got it. For after-care, you've told me you wish your blanket, the cookies you brought, and your water bottle. I usually stay with my bottom for about an hour after the scene ends.

I'll find a quiet place for us until we both agree you are okay to proceed with your evening. Will that work for you?"

Bottom: "Yes to the after-care items. I usually need only about half an hour of after-care and can let you know when I can be by myself."

Top: "Okay, is there anything else about you that I need to know?"

Bottom: "Nope, I've watched you play many times, and I love your style. Let's go."

⧣⧣⧣⧣⧣⧣⧣⧣⧣⧣⧣⧣⧣⧣⧣⧣⧣⧣⧣⧣⧣⧣⧣⧣⧣⧣⧣⧣⧣⧣

In scene negotiations, the Top will want to determine a few things:

- The bottom's physical and psychological interests and limitations;
- Whether they can agree on the purpose/intent of the scene (to have fun, to practice a skill, to do power exchange…); and
- Whether the bottom is someone the Top wishes to play with.

The bottom is participating in the Top's questions, of course, and (at the same time) asking questions and listening for additional information, such as:

- Whether the Top asks the kind of questions that demonstrate they are ethical,
- Whether the Top appears to have the skills and experience to safely take the bottom on the ride they seek, and
- Whether there is the right *chemistry* between them for the scene to have a shot at being fun/enjoyable/successful.

Negotiations may start at a play party, by phone, or by e-mail. If you're playing with someone new to you, we strongly recommend negotiating in person. When you are face-to-face with another person, voice intonations and body language convey meaning beyond the words. Since the negotiation process, itself, is part of the scene, you'll be more effective at building rapport, excitement, and anticipation if you're sitting together, planning the event.

Be creative; enjoy the negotiating process. In this arena, a boring and sterile negotiating style is your enemy. It signals the bottom that there's a good chance your scene will also be somewhat boring and sterile. This is a time to get to know one another and is actually part of the scene. Whatever you are seeking, begin creating it now. *Starting right now (and lasting throughout the scene), the bottom and the Top begin working together to set the tone and intention that can transform the experience from the mundane to the magical.*

If the bottom is seeking a cathartic or spiritual release, you may want to take a more serious and sensitive approach. As one example, you may want to discuss inserting some ceremonies (such as burning sage) and selecting background music that matches the mood you are creating.

If the bottom is seeking a playful, light-hearted experience, you may incorporate jokes and levity to the event. Dr. Bob has been known to bring along a clown hat or a sparkling, flashing pin on his vest.

If you are building a flirtatious scene or a primal/prey exchange, your banter might go like this: "Well, well! You want to play with little ole me? Let me get a better look at my prey. Come a little closer please. I won't bite… at least not until the scene starts. I wonder what is going on inside that delightful brain that made you pick me this evening. Do tell me… Pretty please?" and go from there. Remember, both the Top and bottom are responsible for injecting the energy, tone, and intention into the negotiation as well as the scene. Use your imagination. *If it's for fun, make it fun.*

> Starting with negotiation (and lasting throughout the scene), the bottom and the Top work together to set the tone and intention that transforms the scene from the mundane to the magical.

Behave in the manner that conveys the desired mood. The Goddess (in particular) enjoys a lot of playfulness and sensuality in her interactions (as you can tell by the little exchange she wrote just above). She also requires an undertone of reverence and respect from anyone who wishes her to play with them.

And, bottoms: You're responsible for the safety of your own body and mind. You're being dishonest if you tell a Top that you have no limits ("Anything you wish to do to me is just fine, Sir/Ma'am."). After all, you are not going to do something illegal or unethical just because the Top says it is part of the scene. You are responsible for ensuring that your own needs are met. The more the Top knows about your wants, the greater the chances you will leave the scene with a dreamy smile and floaty memories.

By the way, the Top's needs are likely to get met whether or not they know the bottom's needs. By default, most Tops play for their own pleasure. Otherwise, why would they play? If the Top is experienced, you may be asking them to change from their preferred play style to something different. The Top's willingness to deviate from their preferred play style depends upon such things as their personality, flexibility, and level of BDSM experience. As your negotiation skills increase, the risk of "misaligned will" decreases.

> Unless the Top knows clearly what this particular bottom wants, the Top will likely play the way they usually play. In business, sloppy planning usually leads to undesirable outcomes. Similarly, sloppy scene negotiations generally produce sloppy scenes.

Let me also mention that many Tops become suspicious about a bottom's experience level when they say the Top can do "anything they want" to them. Such a broad, non-specific answer is considered a "red flag." Tops want to be confident that they can trust their bottom. After all, the Top has no idea what the bottom is mentally excluding from the "anything" category. For example, the bottom is unlikely to want to be stabbed, shot, or punched in the face.

Articulate or Tongue-Tied...

People differ. So expect differences between how well the Top and bottom work through scene negotiations. Keep this in mind: **a bottom is not necessarily a submissive**. We both know any number of Tops who like to receive intense sensations and who would bristle at being called a bottom. (They may admit to "bottoming," but distinguish that from "*being* a bottom.")

Top and bottom are **position** descriptions, not **role** descriptions. At some point, you will meet both an s-type *service Top*, and a D-type masochist. ★

Put your assumptions away when you're in our world. Watch how people's personalities influence their play styles. Learn.

★ Note: As an example, Bob lived for many years as a service Top to his female Master who enjoyed what she termed "intense sensations." When playing in the dungeons at large BDSM conferences people sometimes asked us how it could be that the slave was Topping its Owner. The simple answer was that this was an aspect of how she wished to be served. As her slave, Topping her was an act of service, never an act of domination.

There can be big differences between how well the Top and bottom manage the negotiation process. Some people (Top or bottom) are very articulate and are used to declaring what they want. Others are more shy or timid about expressing their needs. Both parties share communication responsibilities.

- The Top must make sure they understand the bottom's version of "no." That also means not repeatedly asking them to participate in scene activities. (This is a consent violation.) Not everyone says "No" the same way. Many people shy away from "confrontational" languaging. "Not right now," or "perhaps another time," or "I don't think so," are all still "No."

- The bottom is responsible for being clear about what they really wish the Top to do in the scene. (Take personal responsibility for your needs.)

- The bottom is responsible for learning whether the Top is skilled in (and enjoys) the type of play they are requesting.

- The Top also is responsible for letting the bottom know whether they are experienced at the type of scene they are discussing. Similarly, the bottom must be forthcoming and tell the Top whether they have experience in such a scene.

Remember: "Luck" is preparation meeting opportunity. Each of us is responsible for being properly prepared so we can create luck from the opportunity that presents itself.

TYPICAL FIRST-TIME DISCUSSIONS TOPICS

This is a list of topics typically covered when planning a scene with a new play partner.

- Logistics:
  - Type of scene being negotiated.
  - People involved and their roles.
  - Time and place for the play scene.
  - How long you'll be playing (15 minutes or two hours or more). Note: In a public play space, it is courteous to complete your play scene within 30-45 minutes when others are waiting.
  - Safewords.
  - After-care. Do they expect after-care; what does that look like?
- Limits:
  - What is *totally* okay to do?
  - What is *absolutely not okay* to do?
  - Physical limits:
    - o duration of play.
    - o medical restrictions (diabetes, poor circulation, hypoglycemia, etc.) that the Top needs to know about.

- o physical limitations (joints, bad back, inflexibility, flat feet, etc.).

- o medicines or medical conditions that need to be discussed (such as blood-thinning medications that could make it hard to stop bleeding or cause excessive bruising).

- o limits particularly associated with bondage—joints, flexibility, physical limitations (such as how long the bottom is able to stand, kneel, etc.).

- ⊙ Emotional landmines:

  - o history of emotional abuse?

  - o history of sexual abuse?

  - o history of physical abuse, especially if there are triggers to avoid such as certain words, actions or toys? (Your honor and reputation depend on respecting areas you've been asked to avoid.)

  - o other types of trauma?

- ⊙ Intimacy level (chests, breasts, genitals, penetration, kissing, fluid exchange, etc.).

- ● Finer points:

  - ⊙ Do they understand this is a scene and not the beginning of a BDSM relationship?

  - ⊙ How intense should the play be and how do they let you know it's getting too intense? Do they want any marks? Are these to be temporary marks or permanent marks? What about humiliation play?

  - ⊙ Do they have new or old injuries or physically or psychologically limiting issues like claustrophobia?

  - ⊙ What is their relationship status (as in, are they in one?) and do they have permission to play?

  - ⊙ Are there any triggers (certain names, such as "slut," "cunt," "pussy," or actions—such as face-slapping or tickling) that the Top needs to know about?

- ⊙ Relevant medical history (surgeries, chemotherapy, prescription medications)?

- ◯ What follow-up should they expect from you after the scene? Some people don't want to give you contact information. If you are able to do so, a check-in the day after play is polite and will probably be well-received.

Now, on to the details. Oh, you thought those *were* the details? Uh… no.

SOMETIMES, NEGOTIATING REVEALS MISMATCHES

Sometimes when you are negotiating for a scene, you'll have a sense that you're just not the right Top/bottom for this person. It's okay to say "no" to someone. You don't have to end up playing together just because you began negotiating with them. Sometimes the Top must declare a mismatch and withdraw; sometimes the bottom must bow out. No harm, no foul: No hard feelings.

(Dr. Bob speaking…) Before I learned this lesson, I had a negotiation that revealed that a lady and I had nearly polar views about what I was offering and what was going to be okay with her. From this experience, I learned to use exit cues such as: "When I play with someone, my intention is to give them the best scene that I can. From what I can tell by our conversation, our fetishes (or play styles or wants/needs, etc.) don't match very well. I don't think I am a good fit. I wish you well and hope you find what you're looking for."

TRUST IN PLAY

We often speak about "trustworthy" Tops; we don't as often speak about trustworthy bottoms. The Top has to trust the bottom to use safewords when needed. More than that, the Top must trust that the bottom will be clear with them about their own scene needs. Bottoms that simply go along with whatever the Top wants to dish out may not be getting their own needs met. Does the bottom even *know* what they want from that particular scene or this particular Top? If the answer is "no," some time for self-reflection might serve you better than instigating scening.

Within our wide-ranging community, the topic of *mischievous bottoms* comes up every so often. Pouting, saying no, or challenging a Top's behavior is a standard and accepted part of play in certain subcultures in our community. It is often seen at spanking or age-play parties. Boys and bois have a reputation for being mischievous. A bottom may be disobedient in order to provoke someone into spanking them—which, in turn, fulfills their needs.

Imagine you are at a party. You see someone who appears to be a submissive—or a bottom poking at their Top or Dominant in some way. Perhaps they are being sarcastic, cheerfully antagonistic, or intentionally misbehaving in some playful manner. Some Tops enjoy reigning in a mischievous bottom; they may relish the challenge of wresting control from a bratty bottom. Other Tops see this type of behavior as the bottom taking control in the scene, and they're not interested. This kind of bottom-initiated behavior comes up often enough that BDSMers sometimes use the term SAM ("smart-ass masochist") to describe them.

Clearly, it is important to know with **whom you are interacting (and what their boundaries are).** *Being an age-player (or a puppy) at an event doesn't mean you can initiate play with everyone around you. Some Tops enjoy this type of play; others don't want to engage.*

So, back to trust and honesty. The goal is that the Top and bottom can play within their skill levels while getting their mutual needs met. To get to that point, each partner must know themselves and their needs well enough to know what to ask for and how to ask for it.

There is a fine line between articulating clear ideas of what a bottom is seeking and handing a Top a detailed script for the requested play. A bottom who maintains strict control over a scene are often considered to be "topping form the bottom."

Following a bottom's scripted scene often rubs a seasoned Top the wrong way. The idea of tailoring a scene expressly for the bottom's satisfaction is considered the purview of "service tops." Many Tops (and many bottoms, also) consider the Top to be the "decider" about what does and does not happen in a scene. They believe it's up to the bottom to agree to what the decider has chosen to offer. It is a good idea to take a close look at yourself to see if your ego or community pressure has altered your perspective about your role in Top/bottom play and that you remain flexible to negotiation and compromise.

In certain cases, a Top may offer to be a "service Top," especially when a newcomer wants a particular experience. Thus, if a bottom wants to experience a flogging, a Top may agree to give them that experience. However, this is seldom a scene; it's usually a demonstration.

Now that we have discussed the broad view about SM scening, we're ready to move on and describe some of the types of play available to you.

PART 2

TYPES OF PLAY SCENES

Not all play scenes are created equal. Some have greater emotional and physical kick than others. Some scenes are exquisitely subtle; an outsider may not realize that anything is going on beyond what they can see. Other scenes are so visually intense, violent, or emotionally disturbing that you wonder how this could possibly be consensual.

The outlook and demeanor of the Top strongly influences the tone/tempo of the scene. A playful Top will cast a scene quite differently than a primal Top; a more nurturing Mommy/Daddy Dom Top might create a scene quite different from that envisioned by a sadist.

Some scenes are fear-based (see Flagg and Soulhuntre, *The Forked Tongue Revisited: A Handbook for Treating People Badly*, Power in Practice: 2015), while others are seduction-based. At the fear end, the bottom may be left trembling and filled with delectable terror. At the other end of the spectrum, you may see only two people talking. However, one of them is viscerally excited and the other is grinning from ear to ear—they got 'em; they're on the psychological ride.

People differ in all kinds of ways. Their personalities differ, their fantasies differ, and their SM play styles differ. Additionally, other factors, such as a person's mood, how their workday went, whether they had a flat tire, etc. influence their scene. Because of this, consider two important components when preparing for an SM scene.

- The Top's emotional state; and
- The bottom's emotional state.

Take the time to determine everyone's emotional state. No matter how well thought out a scene may be, or how well prepared you think you are, a bad day or a lousy mood can ruin the best of plans. To avoid disappointment, it is better to postpone a highly- anticipated scene if one of the participants is under the weather, feeling down, tired, or otherwise unable to be present and open.

> To have an optimal outcome, it helps to start with optimal conditions.

In addition to this very short list of variables, different people have different purposes driving a particular scene. One person's intent for a scene may only exist with that particular partner on that particular day and at that specific time. The next time you see them to play, the changing mix of variables and moods may produce a different scene.

Or not…

Let's explore that one.

In the world of business, there is something called "product-driven marketing." This is where a company makes, sells, and advertises a single product (or product line). If you happen to want their product, you buy it. If you don't, you don't.

At the other end of the spectrum, you have market-driven marketing. These are companies that produce products based upon current market demand. Apple's iPhone is a classic case. iPhones change almost yearly to meet current market demand.

In BDSM-speak, the product-driven Tops have become really good at something specific (flogging, whips, rope). They become specialists. However, they don't have a broad range of other skills. When they seek play partners, Tops like this are most appealing to bottoms who want to be expertly flogged or whipped or tied up.

Market-driven Tops live at the other end of that spectrum. They might say, "Hey, I do a number of things reasonably well. I can add them in or leave them out based on our negotiated parameters."

Neither is better than the other. Some prefer depth over breadth and vice versa.

There are a select few who are expert in multiple areas. Their fastidious attention to detail, capacity for different types of play, and precision in their chosen crafts are found to be swoon-worthy by bottoms who are seeking ecstasy and expertise. Bottoms dream about being in their clutches.

So… if you aspire to become a Top, you might want to think about which niche you would like to fill.

That brings us to the discussion about some different types of play scenes. This isn't meant to be a comprehensive list. It's is meant to give you an idea of the diversity of play within our BDSM world.

Physical play scenes

When you think about BDSM and *playing,* chances are that you're mostly thinking about the physical aspects—flogging, spanking, nipple clamps, bondage, and so forth. Kinky play actually covers a wide range of activities and intensities. When you start, light play can be compared to going out for a walk, medium play might be compared to a half-mile jog, and heavy play might be compared to a 5K race. For most, a 5K race isn't beyond your reach. However, it takes commitment, preparation, conditioning, and coaching.

This section is not going to tell you how to do physical SM scenes. We will describe some of the more common activity categories and provide some hints about why you'd want to learn the related skills. As you read this, please keep in mind that the world of alternative sexuality is a world of tolerance and acceptance. Just because one of these topics isn't your kink doesn't make it *less* than your kink. One person's *icky* is another person's yu*mmy*!

ENGAGING THE SENSES

When playing, we often focus primarily on the implement we are using or the reaction we are getting. However, you can produce a more rich and transcendent experience (and enhance your scene) by judiciously and intelligently throwing in the kitchen sink: adding depth and breadth by activating all five (or six?) senses. (Dr. Bob: In this case, perhaps the "sixth sense" is fear? Master says I have to tell you I'm joking—but am I?)

You will find it much easier to create a transcendent scene when you have carefully considered how to engage or disengage the bottom's five senses. I, The Goddess Indigo, often incorporate all the senses I can think of in order to send the bottom into sensory overload. Sensory overload is part of the process of mind-scramble that helps keep the bottom away from their "thinking self" and submerged in their "emotional self."

When it comes to sensory overload, you can play with some variables. For example, try mixing pleasant and unpleasant sensations; incorporate discordant or jarring sounds even as you are playing Enigma through your speakers. Creatively integrate taste and smell. Add in some heat and cold. You can even go for wet and smelly, if you are so inclined! Pay attention to what your bottom is seeing as well. As any foodie will tell you, visual appeal makes everything yummier.

We mention ways to build a scene and incorporate or remove sensory stimulation throughout this book.

Sensory play (sensory deprivation or sensory overload)

Limiting one or more of your partner's senses magnifies their other senses. This can add a sense of vulnerability, as well.

- Using a blindfold may amplify the bottom's sensitivity to sound and touch.
- Adding headphones (whether noise-cancelling or with musical sound) reduces their ability to hear outside sounds.
- Including restraints could either increase anxiety and dependence on the Top, or can cause the bottom to relax and let go.

Whether the Top plays nothing or something through the headphones depends on the direction they are taking the scene. There are times when they actually *want* the bottom to hear what they're doing. They can make reassuring sounds or they can make scary sounds. Then there are times when the Top wants the bottom to NOT hear what they are doing. It depends. For example, I (Dr. Bob) don't want my bottoms to wear headphones: I have developed a collection of scary/jarring sounds that I add at random when my bottom is blindfolded. Also, I like to use the silence between touches or other actions to build psychological tension during a scene. We're all a little different.

By the way, I (The Goddess) usually prefer a sensual scene with music that sweeps everyone involved into the fantasyland I have meticulously developed. There is no doubt my boy and I have different styles, yet the results are very much the same—transcendence.

Sensation play—light to heavy

Sensation play goes well with sensory deprivation. To engage the whole body, try using opposing sensations: hot and cold, rough and smooth, firm and light, or fast and slow. Escalating sensations (rather than opposing sensations) can be used to ramp up a scene.

While some Tops may be partial to inside and outside vibrators for sensation play, others may prefer a dull 9" chef's knife or a feather duster. Similarly, many players are partial to a hairbrush or two, rubber bands, a small (cold) skillet, or a warmed towel. These can be jarring and unexpected sensations for a blindfolded bottom. "Jarring and unexpected" (as well as "escalating sensations") can be pathways to subspace… the overall focus of this book.

I (The Goddess) don't tend to use jarring sensations. I usually increase intensity and frequency and then disrupt it with sensual and connected touch. The idea is to avoid becoming repetitive, and to keep the play exciting and fresh.

Sample combinations:

1. Sensory deprivation (limiting one or more of the bottom's senses—sight, hearing, touch, smell) plus restraint (rope bondage, cuffs, vet bandage tape with or without calming, quiet music produces a floaty, comforting feeling. This is a sensual combination and can be a good set-up for energy play or light sensation play.

2. Sensory deprivation plus restraint with high-energy music (preferably without words, such as Japanese war drummers—Kodo Drummers—or Australian aboriginal music—digeridoo—or bagpipes) combined with red/blue/green DJ lights helps produce mental overload and confusion. This can

be a good set-up for impact play or some kinds of mindfuck play. (Safety note: These sensory-heavy scenes will not be appropriate for everyone. For example, be sure the bottom is not susceptible to seizures triggered by flashing lights.)

3. Sensations can range from lightly sensual, to the very edge of the pencil-thin border between pain and pleasure, to outright pain. These sensations can be delivered with expert skill either very slowly or almost immediately.

4. Light sensation play can also serve as a gentle starting-point for heavier impact play.

IMPACT PLAY—COMPRESSION PLAY

If you hit the bottom with something, it's "impact play." This includes hands, fists, paddles, the flat side (or the handle) of a wooden spoon, whips, floggers, etc.

If you are using something to press the skin together, it's "compression play." This includes clothes pins, clips of any sort, and clamps. What you need to know is that some of these items don't hurt as much when being put on or when they are on, but hurt like hell when you remove them. This is because clips and clamps squish most of the blood from the capillaries and compress nerves. The area often goes numb. When the clip is released, blood rushes back in, reviving sensation. You can safely leave something like a household clothespin in place for a few minutes or so without causing damage, depending upon the compression strength of the object and where you place it. Always be careful not to leave it on long enough to cause tissue damage. Please take the time to research any play that is new to you. Wooden or plastic clothespins are available with different compression strengths and also with greater or lesser surface area. You can find clothespins with broad surface areas that hurt less than you would have expected because there is so much more surface area for the clip. Test a new clip on the webbing between your thumb and index finger to see how it compares to your other toys.

Impact play implements are graded on a scale of stingy-to-thuddy. That is, you may select a flogger because it's soft and thuddy; you may select a different flogger because it's stiff and stingy. When spanking, whether you cup your hand or hit with the flat of your hand makes the blow feel thuddy or stingy. You can also consider the depth of a strike. Aiming at the surface of the skin is more likely to feel stingy than aiming for the muscle beneath. Please do NOT use an implement to hit people in the face or head, the neck, over the kidneys in the lower back, directly on the spine, on the Achilles tendon in the calf, on the feet, on the front of the lower leg or the kneecap, or in the abdomen. In general, avoid striking any area where internal organs are not protected or where nerves or joints are close to the surface.

People have different reasons for wanting to be struck. For some, the powerful sensations are intoxicating; they say things such as, "I like where pain takes me." For others, taking and absorbing intense sensations are seen as part of their service to their Master/Dominant/Top. Repeated strong sensations often trigger endorphin release. This can result in euphoric feelings—subspace. Impact play does not have to be brutal. "Hard hitting" isn't the sole path to endorphin release. Dr. Bob's personal play method is to restrain the bottom and establish a repetitive pattern with only moderate force. He waits a few minutes and starts over. He does this over and over and loves to watch his bottom drift off into their own inner world. We call this the "stir until done" method. Note: When making a stew, you have to taste it often as you add things. Same here. You have to check in often with your bottom be sure they are simmering nicely.

Some Tops play specifically to induce a cathartic or "cleansing" state. Repeated and consistent strikes can sweep a bottom into states of ecstasy and transcendence in their own right.

By the way, impact play transitions to a criminal offense once the bottom tells you to stop and you don't. When you're still new to SM play, consider this: To be consensual, impact play must stop at the agreed level.

BONDAGE

Bondage comes in many flavors. It ranges from psychological bondage ("Don't move") to elaborate Shibari (Japanese style) rope work to heavy chains immobilizing your every move and preventing escape. In between, you can secure someone with duct tape, Rap, queen-sized pantyhose (a fetish called "encasement"), plastic wrap, or plaster-of-Paris. Do NOT use zip ties. They are too thin (too intense) and you may over-tighten them, making them VERY difficult to remove. (Safety note: If using zip ties, you should have blunt-nosed medical shears nearby.)

There is a lot to learn about bondage safety. Please take classes, find a mentor, and read books. Practice, practice and practice.

People enjoy being tied for many reasons, of course. Some like the feeling of vulnerability, some like giving up control, some like the sensory-deprivation aspect of this form of play. Others enjoy having something concrete to struggle against so they can express resistance. For some Tops, bondage is an end in itself. The elaborate patterns ARE the scene. For others, bondage is only one aspect of a scene that includes other play types.

Before leaving this section, we would like to take a brief detour into BDSM theory.

In addition to skill or competence, the success or failure of a physical SM scene depends upon successfully combining *intent, focused communication,* and *integrity.* That is:

- You have agreed upon your mutual needs and intentions and established safewords for the scene.
- You have discussed whether you are playing by such standards as SSC, RACK, or PRICK (see glossary).
- You both can be trusted to keep your word. (The bottom will actually use their safewords and the Top will respect the bottom's call; the scene will stay within the parameters agreed to by both parties.)

A note about that last bullet: Personal integrity in BDSM play means that the Top won't introduce unnegotiated play into the scene, and that the bottom will honestly use safewords. Complaints from play partners means you aren't living up to the trust you have been gifted. At the very least, this can reduce your reputation to ash. More importantly, it is a trust violation that can harm your play partner.

D/s Role-Play Scenes

Role-play—fantasy play—is a common form of BDSM play. There are ample online resources. Even in the land of Vanillas, people host costume parties and dress up (often elaborately) for Halloween events. Here are some of the better-known forms, to give you a sense of the breadth of activities covered by BDSM play.

AGEPLAY

NOTE: None of the following material has to be binary or gender-specific.

- Ageplay: One person acts like or treats another as if they were a different age.
- Adult baby: Just as it sounds… the adult is behaving as a baby—often below the age of toilet training (and thus may be wearing diapers).
- Big/littles:
  - Big: "Big" can be used in two ways. It can be used (usually by littles) to indicate someone who acts more adult than themselves (e.g.: to describe a Daddy or someone who isn't a "little") or it can be used to talk about a little's more adult side.
  - Little: A "little" can be an adult who needs, craves, desires, and seeks a parental/young-child type relationship. This includes Mommy/Daddy/Parent, and their babygirl (or babyboy, or babyboi, etc.).

- Daddy/girl or boy and Mommy/girl or boy (and all its variants): Similar to the previous description, but they might be in an older age-range (and not care about coloring books and stuffed toys). Again, this is a protecting/nurturing structure, but every-so-often, the Little may get out of hand and have to be *reprimanded*. Sometimes they may be bratty. That's very likely to get them into trouble. Some are princesses and like to be spoiled (but perhaps have to be taken in hand every so often).

- Daddy/daughter or son or Mommy/son or daughter, etc.: This could be taboo incest play. There are many variations to this type of play and just as many reasons for engaging in it. In the past, there has been some stigma attached to age play, as people believed incorrectly that age-players secretly desired under-age partners.

PET PLAY

Animal play: A player is treated like an animal or enjoys going into animal headspace (dog, cat, pony, etc.). NOTE: There is a big distinction between a person playing the *role* of an animal vs. taking on the *persona* of an animal. (In pony play, for example, if you go up to someone *playing the role* of a pony and speak to them, they will speak back to you in English. On the other hand, if you walk up to someone in *pony space* and speak to them, they will most likely act like a pony and toss their head, whinny, paw the ground, and perhaps attempt to eat your hat.) Once again, this is not the same as secretly desiring bestiality. Your ability to understand such wide-ranging preferences will also increase your tolerance of unusual play styles. More than that, accepting our differences will help our community gain a level of unity we sorely need.

OBJECTIFICATION

- Dollification: The "dollification" subculture is a subset of the BDSM world. A doll is a submissive who strives to please their Dominant by being dressed up, put on display, played with like a doll, etc. Every doll is different and the relationship between a doll and their Dom/me will vary from person to person. Not all dolls are sexual. Some dolls prefer a Daddy/Mommy Dom/me-type partner; others prefer a stricter Master/Mistress-type partner. Many dolls—while not being "mindless" in their everyday life—enjoy being able to lose their free will while being "dollified" by their Dom. A doll may be dressed to appear child-like, but may not exhibit typical childlike in behavior. (See also, "bimbo" and "bimbofication.")

- Forniphilia: This is the practice of using a person as human furniture. For example, the s-type's body may be used as a tray, foot stool, chair, table, cabinet, or other item. Personally, The Goddess and I have most often seen this at Leather "cigar socials" where the submissive serves as a human ashtray. However, we've both also been to BDSM parties where a D-type used their s-type as a footstool and such.

AUTHORITY-BASED PLAY (COERCION PLAY)

- Master/slave: slave is owned by (is the property of) the Master/Mistress/Owner. (Note: the "slave" may have a dominant personality, in which case they are sometimes referred to as the "subordinate." This is a military model.)

- Torturer/captive: Usually a scene (rather than a relationship) where the captor "abuses" the prisoner.

- Kidnap/rape fantasy: The target is captured (often a group effort), bound, gagged, and "taken advantage of." Kidnap scenes can be very elaborate and may take months to plan. It is an advanced form of role-play and usually begins with the bottom's request.

- Gender-play: One or more players take on roles of another gender or blends genders.

- Medical fantasies: This involves fantasy play as doctors, nurses, and patients. This might include intrusive exams or fetishized medical practices.

- Uniform fetish: One or both participants don a military or police uniform. The dominant participant often plays the ranking officer (perhaps a drill sergeant with a new recruit, a military police officer and an AWOL sailor, a police officer and criminal, or two military personnel having a tryst). This may also include the fetishization of a type of material such as leather or latex. There is some controversy about exactly what qualifies as a uniform. For example, would a fantasy scene between a "school principal" and a "naughty student" count as uniform play?

- **Forced orgasm:** The bound bottom is repeatedly forced to orgasm. Who would do such a thing!?! (Oh, no!!! Don't throw me in the briar patch!!)

- **Religious fetish:** Participants often act out religious fantasies in costume. This can include scenes such as "confessionals," atonement, forced religious conversion, self-flagellation, a student with a strict nun as a teacher, Catholic students with a Jesuit priest, corporal punishments, and role-playing the crucifixion (including being actually nailed to a cross), just to name a few. Do we need to tell you that using nails on a human being is an advanced technique that should not be your first attempt to top?

- **Prison fetish:** This is role-play using a prison scenario. Prison-play can be a form of uniform fetish.

- And on and on and on...

When you are starting out in this culture, physical SM play and role-play are the most common activities you're likely to see or recognize. Most of us have a great deal of fun simply dressing up in something sexy and playing with a little bondage and a few toys. However, there are some forms of play that are less often seen, thus not discussed as frequently. These are more difficult to recognize. We'll touch briefly on *psychological play* and *energy play*.

Psychological Play (Including Power Play)

While virtually all Dom/sub or Master/slave play has a psychological component, we're using *psychological play* in the sense that the activity's focus is mental rather than physical. This kind of play involves playing with a person's mind as much or more than altering their physical sensations.

Psychological play is one of the most intense and misunderstood forms of BDSM. Unless you're seeing a big interrogation or humiliation scene, psychological play is often difficult to observe in public dungeons. In fact, you may not even realize that a scene is going on. To you, there are just two people talking.

But remember, this is not the world of WYSIWYG (What You See Is What You Get). Yes, sometimes the two people are just talking, but sometimes, one of them is holding the other transfixed as they twist and play their emotions like a fine musician. You'll get the same hateful look if you interrupt them as you would if you interrupted an exquisite flogging scene. Be aware, and always take a moment to gauge *intensity* before interrupting people who seem to be engaged in any way.

There are some light sides and dark sides to mental play. This area includes hypnotism, humiliation and degradation, and objectification. *Mind-fuck* scenes (such as kidnap, interrogation, and rape scenes) are also part of this group. Such scenes usually require long (and often devilishly subtle) buildup and preparation with a lot of attention paid to scene safety and security. As you would expect, *after-care* has to be carefully worked out well in advance.

While you may have heard about edgier psychological scenes, please remember that the "victim" has usually requested the play. People go to a lot of trouble to craft these events and to make sure everyone is safe and that there is no lasting psychological damage. These are advanced forms of BDSM play and are seldom encountered. Remember, if a scene makes you feel uncomfortable to watch, no problem!! Remove yourself quietly and ask someone senior to explain what's going on.

Midori, an internationally renowned presenter and expert in psychological play, distinguishes between a bottom being humiliated or terrified in fairly harmless areas versus being pushed to their limits in areas that hit core values. The former can be a lot of good fun, while the latter is much more edgy and potentially harmful. Most psychological play is "edge play." It is advanced material. Seek a mentor; read books. Take time and do the research to understand how your actions and words can help or harm your bottom. Know you are responsible for whatever harm is incurred.

Physical masochists derive pleasure from receiving intense bodily stimulation that many would interpret as *pain*. Psychological masochists thrive on being embarrassed, humiliated, and/or degraded mentally. They may also seek other emotional states that are commonly viewed as negative experiences, such as anger, sadness, or fear. People witnessing either type of scene might confuse such consensual acts with hard-core abuse. We know it's hard to understand.

Extreme physical or psychological play is just that: extreme. The bottom may appear unwilling; the bottom may appear to be suffering. Regardless of how the scene appears to you, be assured such edgy scenes are consensual and have been carefully crafted. Safety and consent are bedrock requirements for BDSM scenes at all levels in our community. *Consensual non-consent* (CNC, the general term for this form of play) enables the bottom to experience a ride that is seemingly out of their control. That is a very rare type of play that is difficult to set up within the constraints of informed risk-taking. There is NO requirement to increase the intensity of your play or seek out higher-risk scenes. Experienced players will be quick to tell you that you are a valued member of the community if your needs are easier to meet. Enjoy yourself and don't get sucked into false competition.

Even though we've already discussed *landmines*, we need to mention them again. Psychological play (such as a rape scene) can expose the bottom to trauma that can actually be worse than landmines triggered by physical play (such as impact play). Something may come up during the play—some subject, setting, or action—that triggers emotional reactions that are disproportionate to the event. For example, although the Top and bottom may be used to *rough body play*, one night that same Top may strike that same bottom slightly differently or in a slightly different place or use slightly different banter and trigger an emotional reaction that causes the bottom to go out-of-control. Suddenly, the Top is watching a screaming, enraged, or hysterically crying bottom and hasn't the faintest idea what just happened.

In psychological play, as in all forms of play, accidents can happen despite reasonable preplanning. Should you ever become involved in a scene that triggers a landmine, proceed with caution. It is possible that something about the Top was the trigger. Or it might be that the bottom was in a very sensitive place and did not realize it in advance.

There are two conflicting issues that come up at this point. On the one hand, it's important to try to help the traumatized bottom; on the other hand, the Top also needs to know when to remove themself and let others deal with after-care to prevent further trauma. Damage control may be complex, far-reaching, and may require professional assistance. Edgier play requires a backup plan–and sometimes, a backup plan to your backup plan. The edgier your play, the greater everyone's responsibility. For example, many people plan to spend quiet time together after they play. This form of after-care is effective most of the time. But if your bottom cannot stop crying or cannot control a flashback, the Top will need to know how to get them to ground themselves, calm down, and understand that they are safe. It may take more than one person to do this, so every Top should have an alternate—perhaps a good friend or another partner—who can be called on to provide insight and practical interventions.

> Edgier play = greater responsibility.

> We recommend a backup plan to your backup plan.

Presuming the Top was playing ethically and with consent, you both will have to move on in your own lives without placing blame. To avoid a reoccurrence, the triggered person may want to warn future play partners of this potential landmine. It can also help for each bottom to create a list of statements and activities that help them to ground themselves if they become upset.

What you don't do is blame the other person if both of you communicated honestly during negotiation, did your best to play safely and within stated limits, and acted in good faith. Accidents happen. They are not necessarily anyone's fault. Both The Goddess and I absolutely know Tops who have been totally banned from future club events or activities based solely on a bottom's re-telling of an event that the Top swears didn't happen that way. When the Top has no "priors," it can be very difficult to resolve the incident and assign blame. A Top contaminated in this way has a difficult time ahead; they sometimes simply leave the BDSM community. A bottom who has experienced unexpected distress during a scene may also leave the community, no longer trusting themselves to negotiate a scene. Having kink-aware professional counselors is a must so that people can gain greater insight and make good decisions about whether or not to take a break from BDSM play.

Energy Play

Energy play is an advanced topic and is beyond the scope of this book. There is a small but dedicated group of kinky folk who use the energetic connection between people to augment SM play. This world includes techniques for *cathartic release*, some Tantric practices, and Reiki-like energy work. You'll want to find a guide before you even start down this path. We're not qualified to point you in any particular direction.

The gist of this approach is that since energy lies at the core of all matter, and since the body is matter, one can think of the body as a form of energy. One school of thought holds that one's emotional energy resonates with one's life experiences, personal and professional relationships, and belief systems. They further believe all this has become encoded at the cellular level. Neurobiologists (such as Candace Pert) have demonstrated that emotionally charged thoughts and experiences cause the body to manufacture different neuropeptides (chemicals triggered by emotions). Energy play works in this arena.

Quite a bit of energy work focuses on what is considered to be a dance of electromagnetic energy between people in close contact. The idea is that by guiding mental energy with intentional physical actions—breath, gaze, gesture, and touch—one can learn to achieve emotional and harmonic resonance with another. Some believe that this practice has the potential to open up deeper parts of the personality and energetic body. They may also believe energy play enhances a relationship and intensifies or extends states of sexual pleasure. For some practitioners, it is a way to trigger a psychedelic experience without taking drugs.

Some within our BDSM community have learned to play with this energy field. One national Master/slave conference is devoted to lectures and discussions about this form of spiritual connection (Southwest Leather Conference in Phoenix, AZ). This is not an area where The Goddess or I can guide you; we can only let you know it exists.

Part 3

SCENE? AS IN A SCENE IN A PLAY? OH, IS THAT WHY IT'S CALLED PLAY?

We've already spent quite a bit of time discussing the complexities and nuances of scene negotiations. Negotiations can be (and often are) spontaneous. Negotiations can begin at a munch, while socializing at a party, or spontaneously just before the scene. At the other extreme, the idea of playing with someone may be drawn out over many days, weeks, or months.

If you think about it, as soon as there is an agreement to play, the scene has begun. For both Top and bottom, their minds are engaged. The Top is responsible for aligning expectation and building excitement so that the bottom is already in a heightened state by the time the physical aspects of play begin. In our experience, many seasoned players become casual about the way they start their play scenes, particularly when in their own homes. They rely on being pragmatic rather than creative. In our view, this is one of the reasons scenes fail to become extraordinary experiences: They get mired in the mundane. Mundane and magic are polar experiences. Mundane occurs through neglect; magic must be purposefully created. Magic takes work, but boy, it is worth it!

> Mundane and magic are polar experiences.

> Mundane occurs through neglect; magic must be purposefully created.

> Magic takes work, but boy, it is worth it!

Scene Structure

BDSM *scenes* contain a number of discrete elements—covered in the next chapter. At this point, we intend only to introduce a few basic concepts.

There are five key elements of a scene:

- Negotiation phase.
- Pre-scene activities.
- Activities during the scene.
- After-care.
- Follow-up (also called debriefing).

By way of analogy, it's rather like taking a date to a dance. You start by asking the person if they would like to go to the dance (negotiation stage: when and where to meet, particulars of the occasion, etc.). You come to an agreement. When the time comes, you get dressed, pick them up, and drive them there (pre-scene activities). You engage in activities appropriate to the occasion (perhaps conversation, perhaps dancing). That's the scene. You speak as you're taking the person home and thank them for going with you (after-care) and call them the next day to check in (follow-up and de-briefing).

Let's continue the dance analogy for a moment. In the negotiation phase, you also have to determine the particular *kind* of dance you're proposing. Hip-hop? Freestyle? Country-western? Swing? Latin?) and *their level* of dance experience (e.g.: social dancing, studio dancing, competitive dancing). The message is this: If you want future dance dates with this person, you'll want to take them to the kind of dance environment where they'll feel comfortable. Among other things, you are expected to dance to your partner's skill level. That means no hot-dogging. Focus on making this the best possible experience for your partner.

The same is true in BDSM scening. If you want future BDSM dates, you'll want to verify that their wants are within both your (and your partner's) experience and skill levels. Your purpose is not to make yourself look good; your purpose is to achieve the negotiated outcomes.

Make sure you both have fun so they'll want to play with you again.

Before we discuss common terms used in scenes and scening, here are some important concepts.

First, as Guy Baldwin pointed out in *Ties that Bind: SM/Leather/Fetish/ Erotic Style: Issues, Commentaries and Advice*, Los Angeles: Daedalus Publishing Company, 1993, BDSM scenes are built around SM skills. SM skills, like skills of all kinds, improve with practice. Successful skill execution leads to personal satisfaction. This is a good thing.

Second, scenes tend to close the distance between people. They are intimate, authentic, unprotected, vulnerable, naked experiences. As scenes usually involve strong personal bonding, be prepared for the emotional aspect of a scene. In other words, we don't do BDSM because we dislike each other. Topping and bottoming are acts of love (or at least like) and mutual respect.

Third, those who get involved with BDSM in the first place often do so to get a better understanding of how they fit in this world. Intense scenes change us in subtle and not-so-subtle ways.

Fourth, scenes last as long as they last, from seconds to months. However, in a crowded public dungeon, courtesy requires you to limit your play to about 30–45 minutes. There are probably other people waiting to use that four-poster bed, sling, cage, suspension point, or cross.

Understanding Altered States

SUBSPACE

Subspace refers to the psychological state caused when your brain releases endorphins and adrenaline (previously discussed). Endorphins are naturally produced in response to stress and pain. While subspace can be elusive, it is most likely to occur during sm play when five conditions have been met:

- The players trust one another.
- The physical setting is conducive to that particular kind of scene.
- The psychological mood is right.
- The Top's sm skills are being applied to match the bottom's experience level.
- Their kinks match—players get aroused/thrilled/engaged, etc., by this kind of play.

Because each of these five conditions contain so many uncontrollable variables, you can readily understand why many bottoms have never experienced subspace at all.

Subspace is a metaphor for the bottom's mental state during a deeply involved play scene. Many types of sm play invoke strong physical responses. Bottoms experiencing both the physical and psychological aspects of BDSM may mentally separate themselves from their environment (and their bodies) as they process their experiences. They zone out. They lose their sense of time; their hearing is dampened. For this reason, subspace can be compared to a trance state in which the bottom is disconnected from their physical and/or thinking self. Their rational mind is usually not in control.

In our community, subspace has a certain mystique. Subspace feels good. It can be an addicting experience that bottoms seek over and over; it is a natural high. Coming down from subspace can take as long (or longer) than the scene itself.

As an intense scene ends, don't do anything to startle a bottom. The Top needs to gently and firmly assist their bottom to the prearranged after-care area. Being roused abruptly from a trance may be disorienting. It is like being startled from a deep sleep.

More extreme disorientation is particularly likely when something goes wrong in a scene. If the interrupting event is perceived as threatening, the bottom's brain may trigger their body to release even more adrenaline (on top of the endorphin/adrenaline mix already coursing through their bloodstream). That can add a huge dose of fight, flight, or even freeze response to their disorientation. This is an example of how a good scene can go horribly wrong in a heartbeat. If you are getting unexpected reactions from your bottom or no reactions at all, it's time to check in and see what is up.

During play, a Top's ability to drop their partner into an altered mental state relies heavily on two factors: how well the Top can read the bottom's verbal and non-verbal signs, and how well the bottom can communicate their mental and physical states to the Top.

Correctly reading the bottom enables the Top to control how quickly or slowly the bottom will go into subspace, how long they remain in subspace, and how smoothly they come out of subspace—presuming that the bottom is able to go into subspace at all.

For a variety of important reasons, subspace can't be guaranteed. For example:

- Does the Top know about the bottom's mental or physical state when starting the scene? (Did they have a good day at the office? Did they just see someone in the dungeon they've been trying to avoid? Is the ambient music annoying them? Is it too bright? Too dark?)

O Does the Top understanding the types of stress or physical stimulation that can launch that particular bottom into subspace?

O Does the Top understanding how adrenalin/endorphins work on a bottom in general (and that bottom in particular)?

O Does the Top know the types of sensations that will move that particular bottom toward or away from subspace?

O Does the Top have the necessary skills to create a scene that is conducive to entering subspace?

Endorphins and Adrenaline

Adrenaline causes an increase in heart rate and blood pressure; endorphins cause them to decrease. Adrenaline is produced in the adrenal glands; endorphins are produced primarily in the pituitary and hypothalamus glands. They also have powerful natural pain-control capabilities... another reason not to negotiate once a scene begins.

Another term you may hear is "flying." Some people consider *flying* **to be different from subspace.** Regardless of whether you consider them to be separate or the same, they are both *altered states of reality*, and as such need to be treated with care and respect.

BDSM practices can be used for spiritual purposes. A spiritually-based play scene can cause the bottom to fly (or enter subspace). We know several people who play this way. This might mean agreeing that the scene will be spiritual in nature, playing shamanic music, darkening the room, lighting many candles, *cleansing the room,* etc.

I, Dr. Bob, have used spiritually-based play to help my partner have out-of-body experiences. We found that if I touched her about a dozen times with the red-hot tip of a dissecting needle, her eyes would roll back in her head and she would be off on her trip. However, I discovered that I had to be careful how long I let her fly. The longer I let her go, the harder and harder it became to bring her back. Interestingly, she would always come back with a story from her travels to far-away places, usually Jerusalem under Roman rule or to a remote mountain in Scotland where she found herself sitting in a ring of boulders.

There are countless ways to create spiritual scenes like these. In any case, after the bottom "goes away," the Top must determine when they have been floating long enough, and slowly and gently bring them back. It can help to specify what the signal for returning will be (perhaps a specific piece of music, a whispered name, the sound of bells). If your bottom is a regular play partner, your signal for return becomes more effective the more often it is used.

About the Term "Subspace"

The term subspace began its life as the phrase, "the sub's space"—meaning the headspace that a submissive bottom enters once SM play has caused endorphins and adrenaline to be released throughout their body. Over time, it was shortened to subspace. Its linguistic mate is Top-space.

While it is usually a submissive that is bottoming, that is not always the case. The bottom may be a masochistic Dominant (who may object to the term subspace).

There are some play implications of subspace. As a Top, your play will improve as you understand the interplay between your bottom's *emotional* states and *thinking* states. For example, you can snap your bottom out of their beautiful, floaty experience by asking thought-provoking questions. It can be hard for someone in subspace to refocus quickly enough to recognize even that you are expecting an answer. If a scene is well underway and the Top asks the bottom an actual question, the Top will notice a few things:

- The bottom isn't pleased about having to leave their emotional happy-place to answer a question *unless it's safety-related*. Thus, it's a bad idea for a Top to repeatedly interrupt the flow of the scene to ask, "How are you doing?" As the Top, it's your job to be able to read how the bottom is doing without asking over and over again.

- The bottom may not be present enough to tell you that they are in an uncomfortable position. They may not know a limb has gone numb, or that the sensations are too intense. (This is where your SM play safety training becomes critical.)

Believe it or not, there is a surprise message in all this. As the scene progresses and the bottom is approaching subspace, their reasoning ability becomes impaired. Two important rules are derived from this:

- First, it's unethical to try to renegotiate during the scene; and

- Second, the bottom can't always be relied upon to use either verbal or physical safewords.

We have already mentioned some alternatives for bottoms who cannot speak, but will repeat them here. You can have the bottom hold something that can be dropped to signal "red." This could include a neon orange rubber ball, a bell, or a wadded-up piece of paper. By the way, dropping something isn't an adequate backup system by itself. If you have a bottom who has floated away, they may not have the wherewithal to drop anything—or they might drop it accidentally. This is when the Top must be on high alert, monitoring the bottom's breathing, skin tone, body temperature, body/hand movements, sounds, and so forth. This is the bottom's point of maximum vulnerability during a scene. It is your moment to live up to the trust your bottom has placed in you.

A word of caution: If you want your safeword to work, you will have to practice it. Make time to go through your safety protocols in the actual setting before you use them in play. What sounds like a good idea may not withstand the reality test. If you (as the Top) think that dropping a bell will get your attention during a scene in a loud, busy dungeon, try it out. It may work; it may not work. Same with the idea that dropping a neon orange ball is a signal from the bottom. It may get dropped, but you may not notice it. It may even roll away into someone else's scene. Not good. Every time you enter an unfamiliar play space, verify that your safety protocols will work. Loud dungeon background noises (or darker spaces than you're used to) may well impair the effectiveness even of your rehearsed signals.

Often, often, often, a bottom feels they have to "take it for their Master/Dominant." They believe their "ouches" prove their worth as a submissive. We have heard people say, "Real submissives don't red-out." Outrageous, in our own opinion. Honesty and transparency prove the bottom's worth to the Top. How do you get to subspace if your mind keeps saying "Ouch, this is too much"? Trust and relaxation are disrupted by the tension of trying to force yourself to take sensations that are too much, too fast.

Moral: It is important to be sure to have a safeword that is easy to remember. When all else fails, revert to the familiar. Words can fail us, especially recalling and expressing a word during moments of stress. If the bottom can't recall their safeword, we strongly recommend that they use their own name as the fallback safeword. While someone might not be able to remember to say, "Pineapple enchilada" in the heat of the moment, they can probably remember their own name. Particularly when doing pick-up play, a bottom calling out their own name can be the safeword-of-last-resort. You can also simply say "safe word!" No Top worth their salt will ignore that.

The bottom has ultimate responsibility for self-preservation. As we keep saying, the bottom is responsible for knowing enough about the play to know when the Top is being unsafe. We'll admit, consent is a tricky thing. That said, we absolutely know of some Master/slave relationships where the Master requires the slave to reaffirm consent on an almost daily basis. You're not in Kansas anymore, Dorothy.

Speaking of safewords and emergencies, if a bottom is heavily into subspace when an emergency occurs (or if someone uninvited obtrusively enters the scene), the Top will not be able to rely on much/any help from that bottom. In fact, there is a risk that a bottom suddenly aroused out of deep subspace will act irrationally and actually add to the complexity of the emergency the Top is trying to manage.

It is the Top's responsibility to remain aware of all of these things. It is an immense responsibility.

TOP-SPACE

It is our observation that Top-space usually starts out adrenaline-driven while subspace seems largely endorphin-driven. But neither one of us is a neuroscientist, so take that observation for what it is worth. We mean that while the bottom may be zoned out, the Top may be on high alert. (We will discuss this again towards the end of this book in the section on the psychological risks of play.) Everyone is different, of course. You are likely to find your bottom starting out with adrenaline-driven responses but becomes flooded with endorphins by the end of your well-crafted and successful scene. This pattern may be mirrored by the Top as well.

The incredible highs one experiences from successful intense play are so enjoyable that people want to get to that place again and again. They crave and desire it. They may well want to go deeper and deeper and... Both the Top and bottom will find it easier and easier to get there with the right person(s).

AFTER-CARE

An SM scene shouldn't end when toys are put away. Generally, a scene transitions into *after-care*. After-care is generally meant to be the period during which the Top helps the bottom to regain personal control physically, emotionally, and psychologically.

After-care is to a scene what an *ending* is for a novel or movie. After-care rounds out (completes) the scene. The kind of after-care (and the duration of that care) depends upon a number of factors, such as:

- How those involved with the scene are processing the experience.

- Whether quieter areas are available for after-care. A busy and crowded dungeon might not have a separate area designated for after-care, or those spaces could already be in use.

- Whether this is a new play partner (and, if not, the nature of your relationship—social friends, D/s, DDlg/lg, etc.).

- Where the scene falls on a scale from "sensual" to "extreme."

- Whether you're in a hurry to clean up so another person can use the equipment.

- Whether the scene's intent is skills practice, a sampling of the Top's range of techniques, bonding, etc.

- The players' emotional closeness and negotiated parameters (bonded pair vs. pick-up play).

In fact, not all SM scenes end with after-care. For example, some mindfuck scenes depend on the bottom processing the experience on their own. In such situations, a cuddling-type after-care might negate the Top's intent or bring the bottom out of an experience they want to prolong and cherish. Similarly, when a true sadist is playing consensually with a true masochist, neither player might want cuddly after-care.

As PhoenixRed once commented, the bottom may only need to be asked if they're okay. Sometimes they don't want cuddles; they want privacy or, frankly, just to be alone. She added that she knew of cases where the bottom wanted to feel abandoned as they're putting themselves back together psychologically. That very act helped them to build their own emotional strength.

Not all subspace is a floaty "happy place." Sometimes it's dark. Similar to *good pain* and *bad pain,* there are good dark places and bad dark places a bottom can go during a scene. It's up to each person to respectfully get their own needs met and to safeguard their own physical, psychological, and emotional safety.

After some experience, you'll be able to adapt your after-care techniques to be appropriate to your specific situation. There is no cookie-cutter model for giving after-care; it has to fit the situation and the people.

All that said, we'll now address basic after-care for the Top and bottom. This is your general guide for playing safely; it is up to you to customize after-care that fits your needs.

SM play often pushes the edges of your comfort zone both as a Top and as a bottom. Thus, the period following play is a time when the bottom can reassure the Top that they (the Top) did what they (the bottom) had agreed to. Even though you may have been playing for many, many years, it is an important courtesy to thank one another for the scene (unless thanking the other person is not in alignment with your scene, such as a scene involving humiliation or degradation).

The bottom has just come out of a very intense experience; they might be disoriented. Perhaps they can't walk or hold a high-level conversation. They need to be watched a bit until they once more become a competent adult, especially if they are going to be driving.

Now, please pay attention right here. Psychologists say that your most vivid memory of an encounter or event is strongly influenced by what happens at the very beginning and in the last three minutes of contact. In fact, it's been shown that you'll have a stronger recollection of that good or bad ending than you'll have of the overall event. The message: What you say (and how you say it) during after-care will be the memory your bottom carries with them. How you handle after-care will affect your relationship with that person. This is your opportunity to establish a spectacular memory.

Let me explain.

Hypnotists put someone into a trance state by using some form of induction. They ask the person to do a few things, such as to relax their body, listen as they count up or down, or try to follow a moving object. They maintain a special speaking patter in a rhythmic, soft voice. They will deepen the trance a few times. This leads the subject to be more psychologically open or susceptible to what the hypnotist is suggesting. Later (in the section on "psychological risk"), we will discuss how the BDSM states of "Top-space" and "subspace" represent trance states. There, we will explain that what the Top says to the bottom after a scene (particularly after an intense scene) is psychologically very important.

The point of this side-trip is that the term for bringing a person out of an hypnotic trance and back to their normal self is called an "exduction." Tying that to our current discussion, after-care can be considered an *exduction* process.

Here is an important tip—also from the world of hypnosis—*what you say and how you say it matters.* It helps if you reassure the bottom at this time. Don't make plans for another scene while they are still "under the influence." "I am here with you. I am going to stay here until you let me know you are fully recovered," etc.

Do not make statements that could color the bottom's perception of the play immediately after the scene. Be sure you are *comforting* them rather than *influencing* them. We mention trance states many times in this book. Phrases such as, "Wasn't that the best scene you ever had?" or, "I know you are already looking forward to playing together again!"

are not very ethical when you are speaking to someone who may be quite vulnerable to suggestion. In fact, phrases such as these, when said to someone in a trance-like state, can become a post-hypnotic suggestion. Because the bottom may be susceptible to being swayed, any action that considered suggestable is absolutely unethical and non-consensual.

While we are speaking about the world of hypnosis, consider this. Your pre-scene activities represent the *induction* to the scene itself. During the scene, you have the opportunity to put the bottom into a trance-like state. After-care (exduction) transitions the bottom from trance to the present. (Thanks to Master Hypnotist Master Shack from San Antonio for linking the key elements of a scene to the stages of hypnosis.)

After-care is the most obvious and practical way to help combat emotional drop at the end of an intense scene. It's important for after-care to last long enough for the bottom to be able to stand up, walk around, and be rational. This is also a time when adrenaline is draining out of the Top's own system.

More after-care subtleties: The Top's mental state may complicate the after-care process. Most obviously, after-care is as important for the Top as it is for the bottom. Remember, the bottom wasn't the only one on the ride. The Top had a ticket as well. However, that doesn't mean that the post-scene period is always a warm, fuzzy, and cuddly time for the Top. If the scene involved particularly heavy play, a Top may not be psychologically able to switch gears on a dime in order to focus on their bottom.

Intense scenes produce intense adrenaline-driven experiences for a Top and after-care should not be an afterthought. In fact, both The Goddess and I know couples who have a particular protocol that the bottom cleans up the area once play ends while the Top leaves to give themselves needed self-care. In those cases, they may make arrangements with others to provide the bottom's after-care as well as help clear and clean the area.

Translation: Before the scene, the Top and bottom might want to discuss the **Top's** needs for after-care (and the form it will take).

Now, even if you knew that, here is a bit more. This will make more sense as you gain experience with play scenes.

There may be specific and valid reasons why a Top might not be the person providing after-care. For example:

- The Top may have played with someone else's partner (or property) and the bottom's regular partner will handle the after-care.

- The Top or bottom may not intend to build a relationship; neither wants to bond emotionally.

- The scene may have been a demo, and the bottom has no desire to bond with the Top.

In such cases, it's a good idea to require the bottom to provide a friend to manage after-care (if they need it and want it). If the bottom does not want the Top to provide after-care, say so. Ditto for the Top. If the Top doesn't want to provide after-care, say so. Although this may sound edgy, let us be clear: It is *not* the Top's automatic responsibility to provide after-care. After-care for the Top and for the bottom is negotiated, just like every other aspect of play negotiations. It has to be consensual.

If someone else is to provide after-care, the selected person should (must) agree to observe the entire scene, in order to know the intensity level, type of play, responses, etc. This helps the after-care-provider to judge the kind of care most appropriate to the scene.

Once, I (Dr. Bob) was doing an intense "advanced foreplay" class with my Master of the time. She'd squirted all over the place and was flying by the time we were done. Since we knew we had to clean up immediately after the demo because a play party was starting, I found a good-looking guy who agreed to provide after-care. Problem: He now had a mostly-naked 5'7" blonde (my then-Master) in his lap. He couldn't resist stroking her—in contrast to simply holding her. This non-negotiated consent violation pulled her right out of subspace and dropped her into anger. She felt violated. However, we realized it was our fault for not having discussed it with him. We realized he was offering the kind of comfort and support he would provide to his own play partner. However, he had missed a very important step. He hadn't asked either one of us if "stroking her breasts" was okay. Moral: Pre-negotiate what is (and what is not) permitted during after-care with someone else's bottom.

True story from The Goddess Indigo: I was hosting a Black Beat party in Houston, TX in the early 2000s. A mostly-naked female was carrying a sign requesting heavy-duty play. It appeared most of the party went upstairs at one point and played with her or witnessed the scene. Afterwards, I went upstairs to check on the state of the room where the play had occurred to see if it needed freshening or cleaning. The room was completely dark, which was surprising during a party. I flipped the light switch on, and there she was—lying alone on the cold tile floor without even a blanket! I immediately asked if she was okay and whether she needed anything. She calmly told me, "No," and said she was fine. Little did I know, this was still part of her scene. She liked to feel abandoned afterward. My intrusion was exactly what she *didn't* need. Note: Let hosts and DMs know ahead of time if your scene will go outside the norms of usual play. This way, there is less risk that people will unintentionally detract from your hard work.

POST-SCENE REALITIES

Both Tops and bottoms have to cope with the realities of life after a scene. Top-drop and sub-drop refer to the wave of reality that washes over people who have become emotionally drained during an intense scene. It's the kind of emotional low you get after returning from a week-long vacation that was particularly spectacular. Suddenly, you are back home and have to mow the lawn and do the laundry.

People react differently after heavy or intense play. Most people are reasonably well recovered within 20–40 minutes. Some get a bit depressed, some want to be left alone (and even want to sleep it off), while others crave companionship. As people react differently to SM scenes, your best policy is not to get stuck in your own ideas of "right" or "wrong" ways someone should manage after-care. Learn to read your play partner. Ask if you don't know.

Top-drop can be particularly harsh. Often, the Top has to pull away from a bottom in order to manage their own emotional needs. The sharp change from Top-space to managing scene logistics (while having to postpone after-care in order to clean up the scene) can be extremely stressful. For this reason, many Tops either make sure someone else is ready to look after the bottom or that someone is there to help them repack tools/toys and clean the equipment.

Cleaning up: When scening at a public play party, you are responsible for cleaning the space for the next players. Whether the Top or the bottom cleans the area depends both upon their particular dynamic and upon the kind of scene they just had. It also depends upon which person is the most functional. You will certainly see times when the Top is too played out to do much, and the bottom is so used to cleaning up after a scene that the Top just lets them do it.

PhoenixRed has mentioned that when a scene is between established partners, the bottom is likely to be directed to help clean up the space (or to clean it up totally on their own). She goes on to mention that actually, some D-types use the scene cleanup process to help restore their sub/bottom to normal cognitive functioning. That is, they use the cleaning process, itself, as a ritual upon which the sub can focus after a scene. Also, *packing up the toys* gives them quiet time to reflect on their scene. The same may be true for the Top. The clean-up process can be turned into a grounding ritual intended to help them regain their self-control.

When established partners are playing and the scene has ended, the bottom usually resumes their service role as a sub/slave. This is not true, of course, if the person bottoming is actually the Dominant in the relationship.

Closing the scene and follow-up—notes for Tops: Unless already discussed and agreed, it's usual to end a scene, provide your after-care, and then say goodnight. Scenes can be intense bonding experiences and sometimes a follow-up or check-in at a later date makes sense.

BDSM etiquette requires you to live up to the faith and trust the bottom placed in you as a responsible member of the kink community. If your scene is particularly intense, you may wish to ask their permission to contact them a day or two later. You'll want to hear about the good, the bad, and the mediocre. Remember, the Top's goal is to figure out how to improve their next scene; the bottom's goal is to be able to explain what they did and didn't like done to them, so elements can be expanded or reduced in the future. Good Tops consistently learn from their scenes.

Think of *follow-up* as a mutual "wellness check" that includes the opportunity to debrief.

Think of *follow-up* as a mutual "wellness check" that includes the opportunity to debrief. When the Top contacts their scene partner within a day or so after play, they learn first-hand whether everything really was okay. Sometimes the bottom has questions or concerns and—as the Top—you'll want to be available to offer your viewpoint. It is *very* important to listen closely to what the bottom has to say without discounting their feelings or views. If they are unhappy about something, help them through the upset. Not only is it the responsible thing to do, this enables you to live up to the initial trust they placed in you. You can also learn of anything that might leave the bottom with a negative (or even uncomfortable) feeling as a result of the play. As a Top, you're going to want to hear about an upset play partner from that person, not from someone else in the community who heard it from X who heard it from Y who heard it from Z. In this light, debriefing your bottom a few days after your scene is in your own best interest. It helps build your reputation as a trustworthy and compassionate person—and as a safe Top.

The opposite side of this lesson can be seen when a Top mishandles a scene and doesn't discuss it with the bottom during after-care or follow-up. Often, Tops won't acknowledge when things go wrong because they:

- Are embarrassed.
- Hope nobody noticed.
- Don't want to acknowledge or accept responsibility. Or,
- Aren't even aware they did anything incorrectly or inappropriately.

Such a Top may find their reputation tainted within the club or community. We know cases where a Top's after-scene behavior resulted in their being warned or banned from future play parties. In extreme cases, we both know people whose play party behavior resulted in being shunned by an entire community—often forever.

The Goddess has been using a system for almost two decades that particularly applies to follow-up after an intense scene. Once the scene is over and the bottom is home, the bottom is to make some notes (only from their perspective) addressing these three areas.

- Before the scene actually began, what do you remember about such things as room comfort (including comments about the temperature and lighting), ambiance, etc.? Such variables can directly impact the scene before it even begins. This information can help the Top better craft future scenes.

- Describe your mood before and after the scene, then detail your mood the next day.

- As the bottom, what were you personally experiencing during the scene? Don't try to guess what I (as the Top) was feeling or thinking. Tops and bottoms sometimes fill in erroneous details of what they believe everyone involved in the scene thought or felt. The Goddess remembers the first time she ran into this type of "scene-misflection." The notes she received after a pretty standard play scene included terms such as, "The searing electric charge when our eyes met," and "Her passionate gaze ran over my body." It is a mistake to project your own experience onto the other person and assume you know what they are thinking and feeling. Scene-misflection has the great risk of creating false expectations that may well lead to awkward tension between the Top and bottom that would not normally have occurred. Scene-misflection can occur with Tops or bottoms. Experienced bottoms know better than to presume a Top's skill is actually a personal, emotional connection.

Scene-misflection: Projecting one's own thoughts, feelings and experiences from a scene onto another person. Scene-misflection can occur with Tops or bottoms.

How a Scene Can Go Wrong (and What to Do About It)

There is no escaping an uncomfortable fact. At some point, you're going to be involved in a scene that doesn't turn out as you expected. In a general way, scenes tend to go wrong because:

- The Top lacked adequate training. They were playing above their skill level);

- The incident was simply an accident.

- The players were mismatched—wrong chemistry, non-responsive, etc.

- The Top was showing off or chose to play in a way they knew was unsafe (negligence).

- The bottom hit a psychological landmine they (themselves) didn't know was there.

- The time or place was wrong. One or more players were too cold, too stressed, too crowded, hated the music, found the space too bright; the list could go on and on.

Clearly, some accidents are harder to deconstruct than others, particularly in SM play. Here's a tip. Especially as you are starting out, ask a senior player to watch your play and provide some feedback. You may be surprised by the unexpected information they will give you. A supportive watcher is particularly important as you explore new types of play.

Sometimes a scene won't go as planned, but there was no harm or injury. If you didn't know some aspect of a skill (or the skill turned out to be more complicated than you realized,) you now know what you need to learn to avoid that situation in the future. Apologize to the bottom (and to anyone else you feel may need an apology) and move on. If you decide you want to learn more about that skill, find someone to help you improve.

If the scene went wrong because there was an accident, figure out what happened so you can avoid those circumstances in the future. Remember: The Top is responsible for checking the equipment's safety and stability before play.

If the scene went wrong due to *your* negligence, you have some soul-searching to do. You may very well need to make amends to someone— or a number of someones. This learning experience is linked to your ethics. How you handle an SM play error of your own making speaks volumes about your character.

If the scene went wrong due to *someone else's* negligence, you are likely to have intense discussions ahead of you. If you are not used to having honest and direct communications, we suggest you immediately purchase one or both books: *Crucial Conversations: Tools for Talking When the Stakes are High,* and/or *Crucial Confrontations: Tools for Resolving Broken Promises, Violated Expectations, and Bad Behavior.* Both books are by Kerry Patterson, Joseph Grenny, Ron McMillan, and Al Switzler. New York: McGraw-Hill Education; 2004 and 2011. Print.

Let's talk about injury.

Start every scene knowing you will take responsibility for your role in any accident. We engage in many play activities that can result in someone getting hurt. Accidents can happen even when we take every precaution we can think of. A clip snaps and breaks the skin, a rope is pulled out from under the bottom too quickly and leaves a burn behind, the handcuff key breaks off in the lock. You learn with experience to check all of your equipment as you are packing your toy bag, to slow yourself down even if you are excited, and to bring a magnet for that broken bit of key and an extra key. If you don't want to take responsibility, don't play.

But there are forms of injury that can't be helped with a first aid kit or a careful survey of your canes and padlocks. Yes, we are circling back to the *landmine* issue for a moment. If the scene starts to go wrong because you hit a psychological landmine, it will help to have thought this one through ahead of time.

As we've said, you can never tell when you might hit a landmine with someone—even with someone who has been a steady play partner for years. It's not that one person did anything "wrong" to the other; it's that something triggered a past memory unique to that person. Often, the cause lies deep in a person's psychological past. It may be very hard for someone to explain what just happened. Here's a story for you.

One time, I (Dr. Bob) was dancing country-western at a bar in a very rural part of Texas. We danced there often and were well known. One evening as we were changing from our dance shoes to our street shoes, a man we knew well was coming off the dance floor. He casually ran his fingers over the top of my then-Owner's foot. It was an innocent gesture of friendship; a way of saying, "Hello."

She slapped him. Loudly.

Sucked the air right out of the dance hall. We were all so stunned that nobody could move. The whole place went quiet. I asked her, "What just happened?"

"My feet are an erogenous zone. He might as well have just felt me up!"

OMFG. Right out in public in front of our entire community of country-western dancers. How was anyone to know this? I didn't even know this. I knew she had a foot fetish, but not that her feet were an erogenous zone. She also had NO idea she would react this way.

We tried going back, but after an attempt or two, we realized this was clearly an incident we could not repair. It was heartbreaking. The gentleman who had touched her foot was actually our favorite guy in the entire place. We stopped going; we'd been dancing there nearly every Wednesday night for well over a year.

In SM play, when you as a Top sense that a bottom has been triggered in some way, *everything needs to stop. Right then.* Approach the situation carefully and with sensitivity. Can the crisis be worked out at that time, or does the bottom need to be removed from their restraints, from the scene, or from YOU?

It may not be immediately clear what triggered the bottom's adverse response. Actually, the "why" is not important right then. Your focus is to take care of the person. A Top asking the bottom the "reason" for their unexpected response may make matters worse. At times like this, wanting to immediately know the "why" underlying their reaction is about you, not about them. Be patient.

When the time is right, try to find out what happened. They may not yet understand what caused the reaction—thus it may not be clear what to do now, or what to avoid in the future. Fundamentally, the Top needs to know whether they triggered the bottom's response, whether the bottom had a flashback of some type, or whether something else was involved.

We have never heard of a universal formula for bringing a bottom back from an emotional meltdown. We've heard experienced players recommend giving power to the bottom. Ask, "What would you like me to do right now?" If you try this approach, speak in a soft and low voice. It's *very important* that you be calm, neither aggressive nor overbearing. Approached incorrectly (for this particular person whom you may not know very well), the situation can get much worse very quickly.

Now, if *that* approach doesn't work, you may need to involve those who know your bottom better than you do and call a DM over for some help.

PhoenixRed adds: "If the landmine relates to a past abusive relationship where the partner was overly authoritative and then abusive in some way, using a forceful voice may make it worse. They may associate that string of behaviors with bad things happening. The key is not to panic. Keep control of yourself even if the bottom seems to be going out of control. Be consoling and understanding, but avoid getting enmeshed in your bottom's emotions. Try to be the stabilizing influence they can lean on."

You may feel guilty as the Top. *Guilt* moves the focus from your bottom to you. When you're mired in guilt, you might be doing things to make yourself feel better about what happened, rather than helping the person in front of you.

This is not the time to start assigning or accepting blame. You could say, "I'm sorry this happened," but you should not accept responsibility if you didn't do anything wrong. Deescalate the situation and keep them safe until they recover.

Now, here's a twist: What if you believe the scene you're watching is dangerous? There are several possible scenarios.

- *You think the bottom is in distress, but you're wrong!* (Dr. Bob's story.) The loud sound of a bullwhip exploded in the public dungeon during one of my first DM experiences. This HUGE guy was using a 10' bullwhip on a petite girl who was screaming her lungs out. With some alarm, I started to move closer to the play only to be stopped by a woman leaning against a column watching the action. Seeing where I was heading, she calmly said: "If you interrupt Beverly's scene, she'll kill you." Ooookkkaaayyy, then. Asking a few questions, I discovered that the Top was a bullwhip master and the bottom was a Harley-riding karate black belt with a passion for being bullwhipped. Who knew?

- *You think the Top isn't competent, but you're wrong.* (Dr. Bob's story.) If you're watching a suspension bondage scene sometime, and it seems as though the rigger is missing something critical, don't say anything unless you **know** your knowledge and level of skill exceeds that of the rigger. When in doubt, find a DM. Surprises can be really unpleasant, and you're going to feel like two cents waiting for change if you interrupt the scene only to discover that the guy doing the rope work is a well-known national presenter on suspension bondage who knows perfectly well what he's doing—and you don't.

- This particular episode occurred many years ago at a large BDSM conference in Chicago. My former Owner and I were scening about 30 feet away. The rigger (a friend of mine) was explosively angry. The dungeon became very quiet as we all watched the screaming match that ensued. As it turns out, he had been in Top-space when a conference attendee inserted himself into the scene without involving a DM. Snapped abruptly back from his well-wrought scene, the Top's reaction was loud and dramatic. He and his bottom/slave/wife—a gorgeous professional bondage model—furiously stormed out of the play area.

○ *You think the Top isn't competent, and you're right.* I, (The Goddess Indigo) remember a scene where the Top had a bottom restrained on a St. Andrews Cross that had been designed with a slight backwards tilt. The Top was using a very heavy flogger with quite a bit of force. The St. Andrews Cross began not only began to move, but had actually shifted and made a thud as it stabilized. The Top did not realize it and went to throw the flogger again. Some people watching ran up to the cross as it began to fall. They managed to grab it before the bottom fell to the ground. This could have caused serious injury. There are times when you must act immediately, otherwise speak with a Dungeon Monitor or an experienced Top familiar with that type of play. The ultimate guide is this: it's better to have to apologize for acting a bit too hastily than to know someone was injured and you could have intervened.

SCENE TRAUMA

Occasionally, you'll hear of (or witness) an sm scene that stopped abruptly. This can happen when:

○ The Top realized they weren't sure what to do next.

○ The Top or bottom became self-conscious with people watching.

○ The bottom did something to set them off (a bratty remark, perhaps).

○ They didn't know how to slow the scene down to end it appropriately.

Whatever the reason, unexpectedly stopping a scene can leave the Top and/or the bottom publicly embarrassed and feeling awkward. This brings up a slightly different topic—the topic of a newcomer permitting another newcomer to play with them.

As a bottom, don't let a Top play with you *beyond their skill level or far above your experience level.* You're asking for trouble.

Here are some lessons for you to consider:

- If both of you are new-ish to BDSM, that's okay. Have fun together. Just don't be dumb together (remember the Darwin Awards).

- Inexperienced Tops may wish to find experienced bottoms willing and able to coach them through *scene construction* (not only coaching about negotiating but also coaching about how to build—and later reduce—the scene's intensity).

- New BDSM couples might consider asking for some guidance from senior members of the community. This is how knowledge and competence are passed down to the next generation.

- Remember: Not everything in BDSM is as it seems. If a scene is making you uncomfortable, ask a DM about it. If the DM says the scene seems to be okay, then go get a cookie.

We are now going to speak candidly and directly to you.

If you want to have a good, solid corporal scene, you must know how, where, and where NOT to strike a bottom, and also have adequate control of the implements you're using. Magic comes from the finesse that evolves from skill mastery. Solid theory and application must become second nature. At that point, rather than simply creating sensation, you will be skillful enough (and confident enough) that your implements become an extension of your arm and your will. Now you can concentrate on creating *connection*. The two (or more) of you will be intertwined synergistically, working together toward a common goal: transcendence.

This takes time to learn. Skill acquisition is cumulative. Depending on the level of difficulty and your own intrinsic abilities, mastery can take years of study and practice. The most respected SM players put in the time to become masters of their artform. This enables them to create magic in the dungeon.

SADISTS IN THE SCENE

In our community, we use the word "sadist" to describe someone who enjoys causing pain in others. Sadists ethically and consensually craft mutually enjoyable scenes. We are not talking about people who lack empathy and compassion and gets their kicks out of non-consensually hurting people. Our community is grounded in consent, and such a person would not be welcomed or tolerated. The average Dom/Top at a play party isn't there to hurt anyone more than requested. Most of us are just trying to show the bottom a good time by doing what we like to do. Since we probably want to do this again either with that bottom or someone else in the community, we follow a few rules. As The Goddess says, "We don't want to break our toys."

The "public" aspect of public play discourages bad actors. Subs/bottoms are cautioned not to start by playing privately with someone they don't know. Vet a new Top and watch them play with someone else in public. Draw your own conclusions.

By way of reality-check, most people worry about actually hurting someone they care about. "Extreme sensations" are one thing, "ouch" is another thing, and a visit to the hospital is in a very different category. If you are a person who converts "pain" to "erotic pleasure" (sometimes called being a "heavy bottom" or a "masochist," by the way), you may need to seek an experienced, heavy Top who, nevertheless, possesses empathy and obeys the strictures of consent and negotiation.

Some Advanced Aspects of Scening

We have provided a strong knowledge base relating to SM play scenes. We will now present some of the more subtle pitfalls.

DOING IT THE *RIGHT* WAY

Some years ago, Dr. Bob's friend PhoenixRed pointed out that while there certainly can be *safe* and *unsafe* ways of doing things in SM play, *rightness* and *wrongness* are harder to determine. In fact, it can be very difficult to tell what is right or wrong when it comes to BDSM topics in general (and SM play styles in particular). For example, when watching a play scene, you can't know what the Top is intending or what that bottom is experiencing. Thus, you can't really judge that particular Top's play.

This does not mean that you should be silent when you see someone inadvertently wrapping a whip or flogger so that it hits the bottom's hip joint or some other part of their body that should not receive strikes. This is a technique error that works against the bottom's ability to relax. It can also cause bruises that take a long time to heal or even damage a joint or nerves. It doesn't mean you should be silent when you see someone's hands turning blue. This is a safety issue that can have long-lasting effects. However, if you are thinking snarky thoughts because someone isn't playing the way you would, you're heading into dangerous territory. You don't know their "why" or their intent or even what they like. This world would be a boring place if we all played the same way. So check yourself. Are you genuinely concerned about safety, or are you minding somebody else's business?

THE TYRANNY OF TECHNIQUE

The *tyranny of technique* is a phrase created by Guy Baldwin to describe kinksters who seem to be focused on getting the mechanics of play correct at the cost of the connection they are trying to establish with their bottom.

To put this in context, you may recall the scene from the 1981 movie *Raiders of the Lost Ark* in which Harrison Ford (as Indiana Jones) is running through a bazaar in Cairo trying to find Marion (who has been kidnapped by some Nazis). Suddenly, he is confronted by a black-robed villain expertly spinning a scimitar in an intimidating fashion. Flashy and showy.

Indiana Jones freezes in his tracks, quickly assesses the situation, shrugs, pulls out his pistol, and shoots the guy dead. Message: The swordsman was a victim of the tyranny of technique. He thought his technical mastery of his chosen weapon was a perfect threat or defense in all situations. Except life doesn't work that way. He was dead before he realized you don't bring a knife to a gunfight.

Now transport that metaphor into the dungeon. Sooner or later, you're going to see a Top who seems to be **performing** for those who are watching as opposed to **connecting** with the bottom—or even connecting with their own pleasure. In a general way, we caution you not to mistake flash for substance. Many think, for example, that a flogging scene is about flogging. It can take many years before some Tops realize that there can be a LOT of reasons for a scene. Once skills are mastered, implements will be an extension of the Top. Learning how to assign meaning to your actions, and getting that intention to resonate with the bottom, may sound rather abstract. But it is just as important.

Performing in a theatrical fashion (rather than connecting with a play partner) poses another risk, too. It can lead to inattentive play. A Top expresses inattentive play (the opposite of *mindful play*) by looking around the room to see who's watching or going through passionless rote motions of some SM technique. (As in bad sex, they're not "all in," and it shows.)

You elevate your craft when you are able to make "connected, transcendent scenes" your norm. That craftsmanship is rooted in practice and preparation. As Abraham Lincoln said: "Give me six hours to chop down a tree and I will spend the first four sharpening the axe."

Most Tops who succeed in establishing the kind of connection with their bottom that leads to magical scenes are also well respected within their communities. It translates into being a thoughtful, considerate, and trustworthy person. We all admire those attributes.

> "Give me six hours to chop down a tree and I will spend the first four sharpening the axe." (Abraham Lincoln)

INCIVILITY IN THE DUNGEON

We're all kinky—and some of us are kinky in ways that make other kinksters uncomfortable. If you're hearing about (or seeing) a BDSM scene that disturbs you, please keep your opinions to yourself. Give others their own opportunities to be weird. Their kink doesn't have to be your kink. There's an actual acronym for it YKINMK; Your Kink Is Not My Kink. Kink-shaming ("yucking somebody else's yum") is frowned upon in our community. You don't have to be into it, but you should not judge or demean others for not being more like you.

Unfortunately, some people remain remarkably uninfluenced by reason and logic. They believe so strongly in their own views about what is right or wrong that they offer unsolicited opinions about how others should behave. Sooner or later, you'll hear such phrases as: "You don't act like a *'real'* Dominant (or a *'real'* submissive)," or, "A 'true' Dominant (or submissive) would do X," or "You're not submissive enough to be a slave," or "You're not alpha enough to be a Dominant." These "rules" are not worth the ink it takes to print them.

As the saying goes, when you're pointing your finger at someone, your other four fingers are pointing back at you. When you hear someone criticizing someone else (or YOU), you might wish to pause and consider a few things about the person offering their opinion.

- Who does this gossip or criticism benefit?
- Is this helping *anyone* achieve their "highest and best?"

- What are the grounds for their authority?
- Is their authority earned or self-declared?
- What do they have to gain by telling you this?
- Are they behaving with honor and integrity?

There are a few guidelines we can offer you. Importantly, keep your inner thoughts to yourself when in a dungeon. What you say can reflect on your reputation. That's easy enough to understand, but it can be more complicated than that. What you say out loud may get lodged in someone's head. It can put a spin on someone else's experiences that evening. So please be careful. We all have enough internalized shame about our sexuality. Community is supposed to make this better, not worse.

We're going to end this section with the opening paragraph from a profound essay written about our BDSM community well over a decade ago. It's called: *Sorry Manners: Civility and Incivility in the Scene,* and it was written by Chris M and Lady Medora.

> One of the most grave and inexplicable problems facing our community in general is the continued presence of downright rudeness. It takes many forms: gossip, arrogance, slander, ingratitude, interpersonal cruelty, rumor mongering, the propensity to snub, shun or belittle, a refined sensitivity to slight paired with strident disregard for how one's actions and words affect others. It is astonishing, and terribly sad how poorly we get along from the viewpoint of interpersonal relationships. Why a community like ours, whose members strive for a mature outlook on power, consent and tolerance should feud with such violence and monotonous regularity is a true mystery. In our community we see behavior one would never dream grown adults could stoop to. We have seen SM groups who ought to get along fine, bicker endlessly and mindlessly.

PSYCHOLOGICAL RISK

Earlier, we spoke a bit about trance states in a scene. We explained two points. First, that pre-scene interactions can be used to induce a trancelike state, and second, that scene "after-care" can be considered a form of trance exduction. Now, we'd like to go over this "trance" discussion in a bit more depth.

Guy Baldwin discussed scene-specific psychological risk in his book *Ties that Bind*. He explained that a Top can create the magical "transcendent" level in a scene by mentally stressing the bottom through power exchange (D/s), and physically stressing the bottom through SM practices. However, Guy (a practicing psychotherapist), cautioned that there can be unanticipated risks both to the Top and the bottom during intense and focused play.

The risk is that the Top and bottom get caught up in *flow*.

In the field of psychology, "flow" is also referred to as "being in the zone." Without loading you down with details, this condition results when expert knowledge or skill is applied under optimal conditions. (See *Flow: The Psychology of Optimal Experience* by Mihaly Csikszentmihalyi, New York: Harper Perennial Classics, 2008.)

In this state, one's sense of time becomes distorted. We experience tunnel-vision. We may no longer hear sounds around us. Self-consciousness fades away. We are off in our own world. Sound familiar? In our BDSM world, we refer to this as "subspace," "floating," or "flying." It's a beautiful thing.

Like all trance states, it can be difficult to know when you're in one. Most of us have had the experience of driving past our own freeway exit or pulling up to our driveway with no recollection of how we really got there. These are examples of driving while in a trance state. You don't realize you have "white-line fever" or "highway hypnosis" (as it's also called) until you wake up from it.

Scene-induced trance states can leave both your conscious and unconscious mind more vulnerable than usual. Your psychological risk is greater during a trance. In this exposed condition, people may be more susceptible to influence than they realize or intend.

At these times, there is a risk that the Top or bottom may misinterpret some of the sensory inputs swirling around them (people speaking, the wrong kind of music, etc.) and overreact or respond in unusual ways. Some interruption or disharmony that might normally be a non-event can escalate into a very real and significant event. The scene can explode without either the Top or the bottom quite understanding what happened to set it off.

But wait, there is more.

Let's say the scene went just fine and now you're giving or receiving after-care. You're not quite out of your trance state. The vulnerable state—the state you may not realize you're in—can continue past the sm play and linger during after-care. When this happens, the after-scene conversation can carry some unusual risks.

Perhaps the Top is consensually cuddling the bottom. That's good. The bottom is looking contented and spent. That's good, too. Dreamily, the bottom says: "Wow, wasn't that marvelous?" Carelessly, the Top replies... (Choose one:)

- "Wow! You were amazing! That was one of my best scenes, ever! We should play together again soon!"

Or

- "How much longer do you need? I have another play date in about 10 minutes."

Now, let's remember that this bit of information is being taken in while the bottom is still in some state of trance. A casual positive or negative comment during after-care has the potential to plant a suggestion (or memory) that can continue to affect them long after the scene has ended. The first suggestion could bias the bottom into feeling that they should play again with this Top. They may assume there is potential for a deeper relationship than the Top is going to want once they get home and have a good night's sleep. The second suggestion may very well cause the bottom to associate sm play with rejection.

If a strong negative experience of this kind happens early in a newcomer's exposure to BDSM, they may withdraw from the community permanently with extremely bad feelings about it.

But wait, there is still more.

Let's say that the scene ended beautifully. The Top emotionally supported the bottom; the bottom expressed their appreciation to the Top. There was even a closing ritual during which the Top returned the bottom's personal power. They did everything right according to conventional wisdom. What might be wrong with this picture?

What might be wrong is called *The Invisible Collar*. This is a term for the formation of a lingering emotional connection.

The Invisible Collar

Dr. Bob's former partner (M. Jen Fairfield) created the term *invisible collar* to describe the lingering emotional connection between people after a bonding experience that does not end decisively. It doesn't matter whether it is a single intense scene, or a months- or years-long personal relationship. One partner is unable to stop their perceived connection, even though the scene or dynamic has ended.

She coined the phrase after recognizing common patterns emerging from discussions about M/s relationship breakups. In particular, Jen noticed that people who had been involved in intense relationships that had ended with *clear closure* reported different post-relationship experiences than people whose relationships had exploded or simply fizzled away.

While *huge* emotional pain and trauma often accompanies a breakup, it seemed that people who ended their relationships with dignity and formality recovered emotionally more quickly (and with less recrimination) than those who avoided clear closure. In fact, many people admitted that when they had ended their relationship, a lingering connection lasted for many months or even years. During that agonizing time of unresolved separation, one (or more) of the previous partners would want to reach out to the other person. Many people said they continued to think about the way the relationship ended and wished it had ended differently. Almost universally, those with whom we spoke reported that their former partner was often on their mind and that this period was a slow emotional torture.

Jen and I (Dr. Bob) discussed the concept quite a bit and realized that the idea of an *invisible collar* also applies to the way scenes end when playing with people other than regular, committed partners.

- ○ You negotiate a scene. There was great build-up; it was a marvelous experience.

- ○ The scene ends, you each thank the other, and you go home.

- ○ One of you felt very "seen" and "connected" during the play. You want to see this person again.

- ○ The person you want to see is not on the same page with you; they are not reciprocating the emotional tendrils you are sending out.

- ○ You feel a bit sad, as though you've missed an opportunity. Often, you think back to how you could have managed to obtain a better outcome.

That's the Invisible Collar.

Know that every situation is different. The invisible collar is a complex phenomenon. This awkward situation doesn't happen often in play settings, however you should be aware it does exist. We will offer rudimentary advice, since we can't know the nuance of your particular situation.

- ○ Let those involved know of any unanticipated lingering effect(s).

- ○ Recognize your feelings and try to work through them.

- ○ Enlist the help of your support system (and the other players) if necessary.

- ○ If that doesn't work, it may be time to seek professional help.

The goal is to bring emotional closure so the invisible collar can melt away.

Part 4

GETTING TO TRANSCENDENCE: MIXING IN MAGIC

Here is the magic we promised throughout the book. When you think of a magician doing an amazing three-minute feat that takes your breath away, you are swept up in astonishment and excitement. You aren't thinking about the painstaking practice (the science, the math, or the timing) that went into creating such a surreal experience.

Once you master the behind-the-scenes material (everything up to this part of the book), practice can lead you to finesse. Welcome to reliably creating transcendent experiences. We call this the "repeatable WOW!"

The concepts we have gone over can be considered to be "modules." You can combine and recombine elements to build an extraordinary experience. It doesn't matter whether you are new to BDSM or have been doing it for years, there is always more to learn (and new ways of approaching what you know). This portion of the book is designed to explain ways to use a few *psychological techniques* to augment *physical stimulation* during a scene. Overall, this section is intended to help you understand how to develop a *defined, repeatable process* in order to have *transcendent experiences* with your play partners. (Remember: a *transcendent* experience is one that goes beyond the limits of an ordinary experience.)

When you begin your BDSM Path, *power exchange* is generally explained as a temporary state. Two people get together (as equals) and agree to have a BDSM scene within defined boundaries. In that context, the bottom (often—and imprecisely—referred to as the "submissive") surrenders some power to the Dominant for the duration of the scene. The scene takes place, and afterwards the dominant returns the submissive's personal power. Two people of equal standing go on to have a lovely evening, whether or not with that play partner. In this sense, power exchange is seen to have a beginning, a middle, and an end.

As you gain experience, you'll realize that it's up to you to branch out from the general ideas in this book and add your own "flavor" to create scenes that fit who you are as a person playing with someone as a Top or bottom.

By way of illustrating this point, we're now going to describe a scene and includes some psychological components. For the sake of keeping sentences in this section free from "he/she/they" or "Dominant/ sub" or "Dom/Domme" constructions, etc., we will use "Dom" or "Dominant" to mean the leader (regardless of gender) and "sub" to mean the follower.

Note from Dr. Bob: Remember, The Goddess is my Dominant (the gender of her slaves is not relevant to her) and I am dominant to another woman. We have no emotional loading or preference for any arrangement over another. Just substitute your own pronouns where they are relevant.

Please bear with us. We realize that we have already covered most of this material, but this is the first time that we have been able to combine the concepts to demonstrate how they flow together. Also, we're including new details to help you better understand how various aspects of BDSM connect in the context of a scene.

> **Suggestions in this section are guidelines, not directives. Please obtain specific consent from your partner before trying any of these.**
>
> **Nothi`ng is more important than consent.**

If you're fairly new to authority-imbalanced dynamics, you will want to learn something about *protocols*. This section assumes that the Dominant or Top knows how to conduct a little on-the-spot (temporary) protocol training for a "new-to-me" submissive or bottom. (See, for example, Robert Rubel and M. Jen Fairfield's book, *Master/slave Mastery: Updated Handbook of Concepts, Approaches, and Practices*, Austin, TX: Red Eight Ball Press, 2014 and also, *Master/slave Mastery—Protocols: Focusing the Intent of Your Relationship*, Austin, TX: Red Eight Ball Press, 2016.)

This generalization does not hold true for non-submissive bottoms. When a non-submissive Top is playing with a non-submissive bottom, you may wish to approach the experience as a team or partnership striving for a mutually beneficial goal.

When a non-submissive bottom is orchestrating a scene with a Top who is (at least temporarily) submissive to them, the authority/power is still firmly in the hands of the non-submissive bottom.

Starting a Scene with Ceremony

Think of a BDSM scene as a story or a play. SM scenes often represent a kind of creative expression for the participants. As with any good story, the opening has to "hook" you; the rest of the scene needs to be one heck of a ride—all the way to its climactic ending. So here's the question: "What kind of creative director are you?"

When it comes to BDSM scenes, you commonly find power exchange between a dominant and submissive partner. BDSM scenes are usually based around predefined rules. One of the rules is to involve ritual to augment the physicality of the scene.

We did not choose the word "ceremony" lightly. It matters how you start. You are setting the tone. For example, if you start a "romantic" dinner in front of a bad tv show with a tray loaded with uninspired fast food, don't be surprised if your romantic evening falls flat. The same is true of an SM scene. You must purposefully set your intention with your bottom in the first few moments.

For instance, I (The Goddess) frequently start a humiliation/degradation scene by taking the time to "sully" my bottom. They are naked before me; I make them dirty. I've used mud, I've spit on them, I've written demeaning words on their body (in reverse with permanent marker, so it's easy for them to read when looking in a mirror—and there is always a mirror). This sets the tone and gives us our focus. We are intentionally moving away from niceties. It's part of my "mind-prep" process. Such intention and ceremony create our energetic focus. It is that focus that is so critical to carry the mood and tension through to the end. We aren't here for fine dining. I make that clear from the first moment.

How can you begin in a way that makes it perfectly clear where your scene is heading?

We (as humans) tend to remember three things about any event:

how it started, the high point, and how it ended.

You are going to have to think your way out of your established scene patterns to address those three points of theory.

- How will you begin?
- How do you orchestrate a high point (and when will you insert it)?
- How will you end the scene leaving both of you satisfied yet wanting more?

Power exchange can supercharge connection during an SM scene. However, you have to know whether you can use it (consent), what to do (knowledge), and how to do it (skills and techniques).

Important Note to Tops about Scene Collars (In Case You Missed It Before)

Do not EVER ask a collared submissive to remove their regular collar OR ask them to add your temporary collar. You'll be showing your outrageous arrogance and ignorance and concurrently deeply offending the sub and (quite likely) pissing off their Dominant—who was nice enough to give you permission to play with their property in the first place.

The challenge is to put the bottom into a nearly instant light trance-state. There are a number of ways to do this. All involve *what you say, how you say it,* and *how you (psychologically, physically, and emotionally) touch them.* In this case, *touch* may include placing something symbolic (such as a scene collar) on them—prenegotiated, of course.

You're about to read about a "pre-scene" scene. This usually (but not always) takes place in the play area in front of the St. Andrews Cross (or spanking bench or whatever), once you are ready to start your scene. That is, your tools/toys are laid out the way you want them, but you have not yet placed your sub onto the play equipment.

Why do a "pre-scene" scene?

A pre-scene exchange helps move the submissive out of their thinking state and into their emotional state. It is important to avoid saying anything that would cause them to *problem-solve* rather than to **react** or **comply** to a direct command.

FRAME OF MIND

The Dom's role at this point is to take psychological control of the situation as quickly as possible. The Dom's frame of mind has just changed from "setting out tools/toys" to "preparing to start the scene." The easiest way to do this is to demonstrably take charge of your play partner. This does not always mean being domineering or pushy, but it does mean you will be firm, focused, and purposeful. The Dominant can use anything they can think of to get their submissive to recognize their authority over the upcoming scene. If the sub is uncollared, they may wish to put them in a scene collar. If the submissive is already your collared property, consider adding another symbol—something used specifically during that scene.

Warning: If this is someone else's collared submissive, they have been loaned to you. It is not okay to touch their collar or add another collar without their Dominant's explicit permission. Touching someone else's collar without permission is a gross breach of BDSM protocol. Not only does it break trust with the person with whom you are about to play, but if the submissive's owner catches you touching their collar or adding to it in some way, they may end the scene in a fairly unpleasant manner. This is not a good way to begin a scene.

Some suggestions: Open yourselves to the idea of having an experience; don't get bogged down in expectations (other than those set during negotiations). There is risk in expecting something. Failure is now an option. Be flexible. Be prepared for things to happen that you had not considered. At the same time, be curious and delighted with the process and where it might lead. Treating a scene as special and magical will make it so.

PAGEANTRY IS GOOD

Pageantry is about adding extraordinary elements to emphasize the special nature of the occasion. This can include clothing choices, music, lighting, foods, rituals, ceremonies, and so forth.

The pre-scene scene is a ritual. Rituals create emotional memories. The more you stay *together* in the moment to relish and emphasize the importance of what it is you are doing, the more automatically you both will drop into that good emotional state when the ritual next begins. This is basic behavioral conditioning. This is also why conducting a ritual before a scene is really part of the scene. The Top is already starting to affect the bottom's expectations of the positive experiences they're about to share. D/s protocols are your path. A little pomp and circumstance at this point sets the tone for the rest of the play.

To hold space for another, the Dominant must be able and willing to be mentally and emotionally present and yet in neutral. This means they should be non-judgmental; waiting. Once they are present for themselves, they will be able to be open and honestly present for another. As *holding space, focus, mindfulness*, and *living in the present* are all elements of a philosophy of living compassionately, we leave further exploration to you. Scenes become magical to the extent the Dominant can maintain connection, focus on the bottom, and at the same time focus on the artistry and skill of scene-mastery.

NOTE: You may not be able to induce a trance state with a dominant bottom the same way as you would with a submissive bottom: A dominant bottom may not relinquish enough control to get into that kind of headspace. A masochist may put up with attempts to elicit submission because they think they need to do that to get severely whipped, or whatever their preferred type of heavy pain might be. Such a bottom might react better to some acknowledgement that you, as a Top, understand they want physical play, not necessarily D/s interaction.

An aligned sadistic Top and masochistic bottom can indulge together knowing their needs are complimentary. Part of BDSM magic is the ability to enter a space where mundane rules don't apply. This is where it is safe to be as Dominant/submissive or sadistic/masochistic as you have negotiated. Once again, "consent" is the key.

CHANGING THE MOOD

(Note: For the remainder of this section, we are going to refer to a female Domme and a male bottom. It is less confusing for us to do it this way rather than going back and forth between "he" and "she" dominants. The Goddess believes it will be easier to follow the text when we have a clear "she=Dominant" and "he=bottom". No bias… LOL.)

So: for starters, you, as the Dominant, will want to do something that indicates a mood-change to your submissive. Separate "coming to the party, socializing, deciding when to play, selecting the equipment, and laying out your tools/toys" from "starting the scene." One way to create that separation is to use what is called a *pattern interrupt*. This means doing something unusual to derail their "thinking state."

You will find it useful to create a ritual for yourself as a way to begin every scene. Using a ritual helps distance you from the background noise of your daily life to become present with your scene-mate. Wear a certain scent, light a special candle, play a specific song. These can be elements of your ritual. Instructing the bottom to present himself in a particular way can create that tendril of magic that draws you into your Top mindset.

This is a good time to enter his personal space. Get close, close enough to smell him. Smelling someone is unusual; it often makes people feel vulnerable. Go behind him and get close; this is another position that can trigger a sense of vulnerability. Slowly and lightly initiate touch from behind, someplace neutral like a shoulder. Walk tightly around him, then back to the front as you trail your fingers across his back. Place yourself excruciatingly close to him, face to face. Now, lower your voice as you (for example) bring his right hand around behind his back and hold it with your right hand while you grab the nape of his neck with your left hand. Don't yank on his hair (if he has any), just run your fingers across his scalp or caress the back of his neck. Finally, *say something that demonstrates your command of the setting.*

SAMPLE OPENING RITUAL

(Hints: You'll want to practice this in front of a mirror as you work out your own wording. Remember: slow your speaking pace and lower your voice. Speak softly, but not so softly the bottom may miss what you're saying. When you speak this way, the bottom is forced to focus on you. Taken together, these are key elements that put a lot of power into your opening moments.)

> "jack, before we begin, I want to remind you that if you need some time to process the intense sensations we will experience, you are to use the safeword *yellow.* Use *"red"* if the sensations become too much and you want me to stop. Do you understand and agree?"

These statements establish the Top's knowledge, authority, responsibility, and trustworthiness. These are important words to use to establish the serious tone before continuing with the next series of phrases. This wording also helps give the bottom permission to "red out" of a scene without feeling guilty.

If jack merely says, "Yes," the Domme may use a dominance-reinforcing phrase such as: "jack, that would be, 'Yes, Ma'am,'" to which he then replies, "Yes, Ma'am."

The Domme continues…

> "jack, during our scene I am going to be in charge of your body in the ways we agreed. You are now under my authority and control. Do you understand and agree?"

Again, jack either says "Yes, Ma'am," or is admonished to do so, perhaps in a sterner voice.

At this point, the Domme might move away from the bottom. She may hold him at arm's distance by both shoulders saying something short and sweet, such as, "Thank you for placing your trust in me. It's time to begin. Now, kneel and kiss my boots."

The more you say, the more you risk breaking the mood you carefully set. Don't get so caught up in waxing poetic that you lose your audience. You have the option to order the bottom to do something for you. This is a way to assess their willingness to comply with your instructions. In place of kissing your boot, you can instruct them to bring you a bottle of water, light a candle, kneel, etc.

Note: Not all bottoms want to be told what to do. This is an important point to include in your negotiation.

> BDSM scenes are intense affairs. The sub is likely to feel emotionally bonded with their Dominant by the time the scene ends. After all, that connection is a key reason for playing in the first place.

> Sometimes, you (as the Dominant) will be playing with a bottom with whom you specifically *do not* wish to form a strong emotional connection. In such cases, we suggest you pre-negotiate that a trusted friend of the bottom's will be available to do the after-care. This lessens the chance of the bottom bonding with you.

This pre-scene time is used to reinforce how important it is for you to be playing with them as a person. Make them feel extra special, because they are. Once you have gone through your ceremony, place the bottom on the equipment, touch them with authority, and express control. Since "control" is expressed differently by people, you'll have to sort out what that means for you.

> *Personal integrity in BDSM play means that the Top will not introduce any play during the scene that was not previously discussed and agreed upon.*

Play Begins

Get connected. As we've mentioned before, the scene is enriched by stimulating as many senses as possible.

- **Touch:** What areas of the body are allowed? Breasts? Genitalia? Fingering? Stroking? Intercourse? What is being excluded? Bellybuttons, throat, face, slapping, pinching, tickling, hitting?

- **Sight:** eyes open or blindfolded? What can he see? Does his view augment the scene? Does it help build psychological tension? If the area is too bright, use a blindfold to remove the distraction. On the other hand, if you're playing in dim light, you still may wish to use a blindfold to augment the scene. However, once blindfolded, you can no longer see/monitor his eyes for reactions, so you're taking away one of the methods of reading the bottom.

- **Breath:** You can learn to control your bottom's breathing rate by matching it, and then changing yours subtly and slowly. His breathing should follow yours.

- **Smell:** incense or scented candles? Use this carefully, as some people are sensitive to odors while others have allergies. Check beforehand.

- **Sound:** music on or off? If music, we strongly advise **against** music with words. (I know, in a public dungeon you don't get a vote.)

- On the music front, I (Dr. Bob) tend towards Japanese Taiko drummers, Australian didgeridoo, or Scottish bagpipe music. The Goddess prefers sensual music with some bass, such as

Enigma, or the Matrix soundtrack. Our music suggestions have two common threads. They have a driving beat and very few words. Such music adds a sense of mystery to the scene. Also—importantly—the heavy beats can help you time your play. When you strike a person in time to music, it can help them go into trance—which is, for many, part of the path to subspace.

FOCUS ON READING THE BOTTOM...

(The more you know of this, the better.)

- What sounds is he making? Does it sound as though he is wholly involved with the play or still in his head? (Higher-pitched sounds often indicate the person is in their *head,* while lower-pitched sounds generally indicate the person is responding from their gut or *visceral core.*) When sensations are new, the bottom is likely to stay in his head as he tries to assess whether he likes them or not.

- Is he moving his body (or part of his body) toward or away from you? If he seems to be moving *away* from you, that could mean that he wants a lighter touch, or he doesn't like what you're doing. Of course, sometimes "moving away" means the bottom is on the brink or culmination of something amazing. You will have one disappointed bottom if you stop. We'd suggest you check for other signs that can make it clear whether what you are doing with this person is being well received or not.

- What's going on with hands/fingers and feet/toes? Are their fingers relaxed or pointed straight out? Hands clenched or open? Legs relaxed or flexed? Toes relaxed or curled? As behaviors such as these are highly individualized, Tops have to learn what these signals mean for each person with whom they play.

- Color of fingers (particularly if bondage or inversion is involved): pink, red, purple. (NOTE: You can use a simple test for what is called *capillary refill response.* If the bottom's fingernails or toes are unpainted, squeeze the tip of a digit until it turns white, release the pressure, and judge the time required for the finger or toe to regain proper color. If it takes more than two seconds, you may have a circulation problem. If their fingernails or toes are painted, judge it from the pad of their finger.) This is particularly true when the bottom's hands are cuffed overhead or when tied for long periods with rope. Presumably, they would have told you during negotiations if they had any circulatory challenges. (Note: Goddess Indigo… As a Black and Asian woman, I am particularly sensitive to the fact that capillary refill response isn't always easy to read. When playing with a canvas richer in melanin, take care to note the temperature of the skin before and during play.)

- What is their breathing pattern? Deep and slow (relaxed) or rapid and shallow (excited, about to climax, or perhaps upset)?

- Holding their breath? Some people hold their breath just as they are about to climax. Depending on how sadistic you are, you can use this as a signal to interrupt their orgasm as part of an orgasm–denial scene.

- Responsiveness: If you're worried that your bottom is not responding as you had expected, check in. Is the bottom still connected with your play? If not, why not? Has something happened to snap the bottom out of a receptive headspace (such as an upsetting flashback)? Does the bottom have anything to tell you (such as, "The knot you tied in the middle of my back is annoying me and bringing me out of my headspace.")? Some people are much less responsive than others. Knowing that can help you better gauge where you are in your journey with your bottom.

Do you remember when you got super close at the beginning of the scene? Use this judiciously during the scene. Get close enough to repeat some of the steps previously used (nape of neck, breath on the skin, etc.). Use that same tone of voice sporadically. Make sure to be in their personal space in pleasurable ways. This is the time for intimacy and closeness. Skin-on-skin contact releases oxytocin. A caress can be as dominant as a smack.

Technique reminder for Tops (we know; we keep saying this—it's important.): Should your bottom start to go into subspace, you have to be careful not to do anything (or say anything) that would cause them to *think*. As previously covered, when someone goes into subspace, they are floating among their feelings. If you ask them a question or do something jarring, you'll pull them into their head ("thinking state") as they try to figure out what you said or what is happening. It can be a scene-stopper.

But—you may *want* a "scene-stopper." Not all scenes are intended to end with the bottom in subspace. In *tease and denial* scenes, for example, orgasm may not be the goal. In fact, the goal might be to frustrate the bottom by *preventing* him from reaching his orgasm.

KEEP THE BOTTOM FROM BECOMING DESENSITIZED

Sometimes you want to keep repeating a pattern without stopping to produce a cathartic climax (see Glossary) or to produce intense pain. Other times you want to change what you're doing in order to continue building the overall scene. You will develop your own techniques as you gain experience and confidence with your SM play.

Here, we'll share some of our "pattern-interrupt" techniques:

- Consider throwing some of Dr. Bob's favorite startling sensations into the scene to help disorient the bottom.
  - Spray water on their back.
  - Use a large piece of tanned leather hide as a flogger.
  - Slap with the flat of your hands, fingers splayed—lots of noise and not much pain.
  - Hold a bit of ice over their body and let it ssssllllloooowwwwlllly drip, drip, drip.
  - Keep some 6-15" strips of 1" foam insulation handy. It makes a VERY LOUD cracking sound when broken over your knee.
  - Have a good-sized sheet of thin metal nearby. Rattled, it sounds like thunder. As you're in the middle of play, the bottom wouldn't have expected the sound of thunder. At least, not next to their ear.

- Use various non-repetitive patterns and levels of intensity to deepen the trance. If your bottom begins to sense a pattern and starts to think about what they are anticipating will happen next, they have left their focus in the present and entered thoughts of the future such as, "Now she's going to switch from the *Bunny* flogger to the heavy duty flogger," or "She's been playing for about 30 minutes now, so she's going to move to another part of my body." This is not where you want them, psychologically. You want them *feeling*, rather than thinking. So go:

  - Fast to slow to quiet.

  - Use a rain stick or other musical, rattling sound.

- Use repetitive patterns and intensities to deepen the trance. Yes, we know that we just said the opposite. However, this can be an intentional way of playing. Part of our point is that you have to know what technique to use at a particular time with a particular bottom. In this case, when the bottom senses there is an unceasing rhythm, they can get out of their mind and surrender to the repetitive stimulation. This is one of the paths to cathartic release. As an example, you can induce a cathartic reaction after flogging at medium intensity for a long time.

NOT ALL BOTTOMS GO INTO TRANCE EVERY TIME

Some people are more susceptible to trance states than others. Similarly, some are more willing than others to have this type of experience. For some, even an intense scene will have little or no psychological impact; the bottom simply enjoys a specific set of physical sensations. There will be a range of reactions from those with whom you are scening.

Message: There are no standard responses in SM play. Don't just focus on the destination; enjoy the journey.

Play Scene Ends

Ending styles vary, but (as we've already mentioned a time or two) you want to avoid a abrupt stop—that is too jarring and psychologically upsetting for the bottom. Also, suddenly stopping a scene is not proper BDSM etiquette. You're supposed to be in control; you need to demonstrate that you're the one who purposefully ended the scene just when you wanted it to end.

You have prepared for the scene to end.

- You have accomplished the purpose of the scene.

- You have read your bottom and know how to deliver an ending that meets your needs, the bottom's needs, and provides clear closure.

- Items needed for the negotiated after-care are set up or easily accessible.

Water is important for both of you during and after a play scene, but you already knew that. Here are some related points. Placing a blanket or robe on (or around) your bottom can symbolically communicate three very different things.

- I'm giving you something to protect you and make you feel less vulnerable (because the scene is over).

- I'm here to provide protection and care as you return to "normal" headspace.

- Here is a blanket (or robe) to cover yourself now that the scene is over.

At some point, after-care signals the bottom's return to autonomy.

Note: If you forgot about having water handy and you're actively taking care of your bottom, we'd suggest you catch the eye of someone watching the scene and ask them to bring you a bottle of water. Water is generally available at public play parties.

> In Top/bottom play, if you've been playing with a submissive bottom (as opposed to Topping another Dominant), it is important to return power back to them lest they now look to you as being THEIR Dominant as opposed to being a Dominant with whom they just had a scene.
>
> As we say repeatedly throughout this book, BDSM scenes are intensely emotional and potentially create strong bonds between people. You can use this emotional power intentionally and with integrity to supercharge your relationship or you can use them carelessly and risk causing emotional damage.

Here are some reminders of things we've said earlier in this book:

- If you are at a play party, don't play for 40 minutes and then continue to occupy the play space for another 20 minutes cuddling the bottom. That is not appropriate, as others are waiting for that space for their own play. Similarly, don't continue to stand in (or very near) the play station coiling your bondage rope (or putting toys away). You're interfering with the next participants' ability to get into their own headspace for their own scene.

- The bottom's recovery time varies. If you've just completed a heavy scene that dropped the bottom into a long period of subspace, plan on spending 20+ minutes on after-care. Everyone processes differently. Be flexible and provide the care required in the way that resonates with the bottom.

- Once your scene has ended, it is the Top's responsibility to be sure the tools/toys have been put away, the area cleaned, and the play furniture is wiped down.

Earlier, we mentioned that when starting out in this culture, *power exchange* is generally seen as a temporary state. Two people get together as equals and agree to have a BDSM scene with defined boundaries. The bottom surrenders power to the Top for the duration of the scene.

Afterwards, the Top returns the bottom's power. Two people of equal personal power go on to have a lovely evening. Power exchange (for the purpose of a scene) has a beginning, a middle, and an end.

Now, if this person is not *your own* submissive, design the closing ritual to leave no doubt that they do **not** belong to *you*. If this bottom belongs to someone else, courtesy requires you to return the undamaged bottom to their rightful partner and thank that person in front of the bottom for permitting you to play with them.

If your bottom is your own submissive, the closing scene can represent a transition away from the play area and back to the social area.

Closing Ritual—After the Bottom Is Up and About

We're about to give you a simple example of a closing ritual. This example applies mainly to people who have only a *play* relationship. That is, they are *not* in a D/s or M/s dynamic with one another. As previously mentioned, in M/s or D/s relationships, if able, the sub returns to *service mode* once their scene has ended and helps put tools/toys away and wipe down the dungeon equipment.

#################################

If you began the scene with an opening procedure designed to establish your dominance, consider some kind of closing procedure that brings the bottom solidly back to equilibrium. We mention this because a clear closing procedure officially ends any power exchange used to begin the scene. Also, this provides an opening for the Top to say supportive and positive things to the bottom.

We coach Tops to insert their closing ritual once after-care is complete. We further encourage them to mirror the style of their opening ritual (as just mentioned). This gives the entire scene a defined ending. So, if the scene began with an embrace, you should now repeat that embrace. If you followed the "close-up" steps we listed earlier, we recommend you again get close, face-to-face. Look them in the eyes (with a smile) then slowly step back to your usual distance for personal space. After you have physically established that distance, say something such as:

> "jack, you were amazing. Thank you for this scene—and thank you for helping to put our tools away and for cleaning the St. Andrews cross. I appreciate our time together. Now, I want to

make sure that you are okay. Do you feel you are in control and able to exercise your personal power?

In the larger sense, when you close a screen by ritualistically mirroring the scene's beginning, that signals the bottom that their trip is over. "The Eagle has landed," as it were.

Past this point, your own personality and social skills guide what you say and do. Let us again admonish you that this is not the time to propose another play date or begin negotiating your next encounter.

Power exchange (for the purpose of a scene) has a beginning, a middle, and an end. If you leave one of these elements unaddressed, the scene may feel a bit "off" when you think back on it.

Debriefing and Scene Report

Earlier, we mentioned (and described in detail) these final stages of the overall scene.

If negotiated and appropriate, contact your play partner a few days after the scene to hear their reactions. Remember, it's important not to lead the de-briefing; it should be from their viewpoint. Be careful to listen with an open heart, as you can learn a great deal about yourself, your play partner, and your scene-mastery.

Part 5

SOME CONCLUDING REMARKS

Summarizing...

TOPPING AND BOTTOMING

During intense scenes, Topping frequently produces adrenaline while bottoming often leads to a release of a mixture of endorphins and adrenaline (depending on what the bottom is experiencing). The fight-or-flight reaction to adrenaline release is relevant to the Top/bottom experience. The unfettered Top may be in adrenaline-produced top-space, while the (often bound) bottom may be in an adrenaline-induced *flight* headspace that could cause their brain to release endorphins. As a result, the Top is *in the zone* and the bottom is in *subspace*. As a Top, you'll know you've reached skill-mastery when this process—the ability to control your headspace while dropping a bottom into subspace—becomes a "defined repeatable process" (whether or not your bottom is a regular play partner).

SKILL MASTERY AND SAFETY

We don't usually speak in absolutes, and when we do, we encourage you to pay attention. Warning: An "absolute" is coming.

You must absolutely master skills that interest you and the safety techniques for those skills. From there, you have the option of learning how to move your connection to a spiritual level. You're not just spanking someone. You're not just flogging someone. You're not just sticking needles in someone. You are learning the skills of your craft. It matters whether you can use a flogger without "wrapping" the bottom. It matters that you can read a bottom well enough to recognize when they have almost reached "yellow" or "red." It matters that you stop before the bottom is about to "red out."

We tend to focus on the skills and techniques of BDSM and forget why we learned them in the first place. This is not surprising, as people tend to learn the "how" of something and miss the "why" of it. However, in this world of alternative sexuality, there's a "why" to all this. Yes, you may have to do some digging to understand what "this" is. We've been describing how you can get to the spiritual bridge between a Top and a bottom through SM play. Once you've established that level of connection, the question is whether you know what do with it. Do you know how to go further? It's a similar problem to that faced by a dog who chases a car and actually catches it. What does a dog do with a car?

However mild or intense your SM scene, it is simply a way to interact and connect with another person. Learn your skills and hone your techniques and, once mastered, apply your mastery to give one another ecstatic experiences.

If you are in a 24/7 dynamic, you have the opportunity to craft a fresh, new scene with your partner(s) daily. You can, in fact, make every morning, noon, and night different, invigorating, and exciting. It's up to you, your imagination, and your wallet. Want to add some interest to your evening meal? How about tying your s-type to their chair? Want to get your D-Type's attention at dinner? Consider serving dinner naked or making yourself the serving platter.

You have now read this book. The next stage is on you. Practice and imagination fall on your side of the ledger. Adapt the skills and knowledge you have learned and bring them to life with your imagination. Now you have the makings of magic.

However, are you taking advantage of the opportunities to make that magic happen? We believe TV is not your friend. Distractions of all kinds are enemies of close relationships. Imagine having 4-5 open hours with your partner every night *without* your usual escapes: TV, phone aps, or video games! What could you do with that time that could make you a more interesting or more educated person? What could you do with that time if you and your partner were a team instead of two individuals? If this paragraph sings to you, you may wish to explore Master/slave relationship structures.

The further you advance in this BDSM world, the more you will realize that personal integrity, skill-mastery, and safe play are among the guiding values shared by those who have remained for decades in the BDSM scene. You will be included or excluded from your community based on your reputation. The more senior you become, the more you are watched and judged. That means that once you start playing publicly, your core values will be on display beyond those in your social circle. After a few years, you can look at those who associate themselves with you and see yourself. Some people will be enveloped in love and respect; for others, not so much.

By the way—for bottoms reading this book—skill mastery also applies to you. Read *The New Bottoming Book* by Dossie Easton and Janet Hardy, Emeryville, California: Greenery Press, 2001. Understand your roles and responsibilities in play. You have an obligation to your Top to communicate both verbally and nonverbally. Learn enough about the activities you want done to know when a Top is (or is not) playing safely. Bottoms: You have a responsibility for self-preservation. Before turning your body over to someone, please find others who can verify that this particular Top is ethical and knows a lot about the activity being proposed.

SCENES ARE INTENSE EXPERIENCES

Intense scenes tend to close the distance between people. They are intimate, authentic, unprotected, vulnerable, naked experiences. When you first start playing, emotional vulnerability can be a psychological hurdle. The bottom is usually naked while the Top is usually clothed; that can be quite an impediment in its own right, as it's contrary to most vanilla party experiences. Overcome these barriers and allow yourself to step outside of your comfort zone. The result can be both freeing and exhilarating. There is an entire world out there to explore. Which is why this kind of "playing" is so much fun!!

Wishing you well...

We have to end the book at some point and you now have the majority of our good ideas about this topic. We hope you enjoyed your time with us and choose to explore our other books, for they, too, are packed with engaging approaches and ideas for living in our kinky world.

We certainly hope you've benefited from this book and are able to use our material to make your BDSM life more solid, stable, and interesting. Our steadfast goal is to provide our community (you) with sound resources to help you thrive, promote your growth, and sustain your passion for WIITWD. Best wishes on your journey.

We welcome comments and encourage you to send Fetlife friend requests.

TheGoddessIndigo and Dr_Bob

Supplementary Materials

Glossary

About the Authors

      Robert J. Rubel (Dr. Bob)

      The Goddess Indigo

Books by Dr. Bob, Solely or with Others

      Books by Robert J. Rubel and M. Jen Fairfield

      Other Books or DVDs by Robert J. Rubel

Glossary

A word to you before you start down this list.

We are absolutely NOT saying these are universally accepted explanations of terms. We write a lot, and in order to be congruent through the books we use certain words to mean specific things. You may not agree with the way we use a word or phrase. We support your own definition of that word or phrase. This is simply a list of words and the way we use them in our books, lectures, and articles.

Anchors / anchoring: From the world of NLP and hypnosis. One use for anchoring is establishing a trigger for an emotional state. If you successfully establish a trigger, you can reproduce that emotion later.

After-care: A scene doesn't end when the toys are put away. After-care describes a period at the close of a scene when each partner can reaffirm the other as they regain physical and mental control of themselves. HOWEVER, not all scenes end in after-care. If you're doing a dungeon scene and there are people waiting for your station, you and your bottom may need to immediately clean up the area. If you know this will be the case and you're not playing with your regular partner, you might wish to arrange for "after-care" to be handled by someone the bottom knows well. Similarly, a degradation scene might not involve after-care, nor might a scene between a sadist and a masochist.

Age-players: Age-players adopt the headspace of someone older or younger than their chronological age, or act as a caretaker/parent to someone role-playing a different age. Common roles are littles, baby-girls, baby-boys, middles, Bigs and parent.

Authority-based relationships: Relationships where one person is clearly the leader and the other is clearly subordinate. Below are some common forms of such relationships. This book mostly describes D/s connections.

- Dominant/submissive (D/s)
- Master/slave (M/s) — Sometimes referred to as TPE, Total Power Exchange
- Owner/property (O/p)

BDSM represents a continuum of practices and expressions, both erotic and non-erotic, involving restraint, sensory stimulation, role-playing, and a variety of interpersonal dynamics. The term "BDSM" is an abbreviation of: **B**ondage/**D**iscipline; **D**ominance/**s**ubmission; **S**ado**M**asochism.

Boi (plural, *bois*): Slang within LGBTQ, butch and femme communities for some submissive, masculine identities. In some lesbian communities, there is an increasing acceptance of variant gender expression, as well as accepting people assigned female at birth (AMAB) who identify as a *boi*. The term *boi* may be used to denote a number of other sexual orientations and possibilities that are not mutually exclusive:

- A boyish lesbian.
- A submissive butch in the BDSM community.
- A young trans man, or a trans man who is in the earlier stages of transitioning.
- A younger bisexual or gay person who may have effeminate characteristics. The term can also be used by anyone who wishes to distinguish from heterosexual or heteronormative identities.

Bois may prefer a range of pronouns, including "he," "she," or nonbinary and gender-neutral pronouns such as "they."

boy: A male submissive partner, defined not by age, but by his obedient role. "boy" is sometimes used as an alternative appellation for "slave."

bottom: The person *receiving* the action (see also: Top).

Catharsis, cathartic release, cathartic climax: Bottom line—the bottom is crying. "Cathartic release" means an emotional release. Catharsis is the purification and purgation of emotions—particularly pity and fear.

Colors: In SM play following SSC (Safe, Sane, and Consensual) rules, the bottom is to signal "yellow" when they need to slow the scene down (perhaps to process the sensations they are receiving) or to alert the Top to some physical distress (perhaps a knot is slipping or is bringing the bottom out of scene headspace). "Red," when called after first calling "yellow," tells the Top to stop the scene, that the bottom has taken all they can. When a bottom calls "red" without any prior indication that there is a problem (e.g.: didn't first call "yellow"), the Top may become angry and decline to continue the scene on the grounds that the bottom was not being honest about their limits given the scene's intensity.

CNC: In the BDSM community, CNC stands for consensual non-consent, also known as rape play. Although it varies scene to scene, it's usually an extreme power exchange where, according to previous negotiation, there is a victim overcome by a predator using force. People who enjoy this play often enjoy either the extreme lack of control or extreme control on either side of the exchange. This type of scene does not encourage ACTUAL rape. All proper scenes are done after much negotiation **between of-age, consenting adults.**

Dominant and submissive (Dom and sub or D-type and s-type) are terms that relate to behaviors linked to personality traits; you could as easily substitute the terms *leader* and *follower*.

Dom and Domme: The shorthand male and female version of the word *dominant*. Generally, when we write "Dom" the person can be of either gender. We use "Domme" when the topic specifically concerns a female dominant. Note: Being a dominant is not to be confused with being domineering.

Daddy Dom: A dominant male who offers a nurturing relationship to his partner (usually but not always his submissive). "DDlg" stands for Daddy Dom/little girl. Sometimes the submissive may be a "little," sometimes not. While Dominant/submissive (D/s) structures *may* be nurturing, the DDlg relationship is specifically designed that way.

D/s play or D/s scenes: Play/scenes (terms we use interchangeably) with or without SM toys/tools that involve the power exchange component of dominance and submission. This includes physical play, psychological play, and role-play.

D/s scenes with sadistic/masochistic preferences—Combining: A *dominant* (Dom or D-type) and a *submissive* (sub or s-type) may have either sadistic or masochistic erotic preferences. Most commonly, those with dominant personalities *give* strong sensations to others, but every so often you will find a strong D-type who has connected sexual pleasure from *receiving* those strong (possibly painful) sensations.

Dungeon Monitor (DM): A Dungeon Monitor (sometimes referred to as a *Dungeon Master* or simply a *DM*) is a person charged with supervising a playspace (or *dungeon*) at BDSM events such as play parties and fetish clubs. While on duty, they monitor the safety of all participants and their authority is absolute. They can stop your scene; they can have you removed from the party. If you are concerned about some activity at a party, it is better to bring it to a DM's attention than to interrupt someone else's scene.

Edging: A sexual D/s term meaning the act of bringing a man or woman up to the edge of orgasm and then keeping them there— often as they are begging for release.

Edgeplay: This word is used in two ways. First, to refer to SM play that is on the edge of someone's personal limits; and second, to refer to SM play that falls into one of two categories:

- Category one—requires advanced training: "You'd better be well trained before you try this one."

- Category two—It's seriously taboo: "You'd better lower your voice before discussing that one."

Emotional Triggers (Landmines): Words or situations that cause an unexpected and often emotionally intense reaction as a result of some prior (and often suppressed) traumatic experience.

Energy Play: The voluntary exchange of subtle energy between two or more people. Usually—but not always—accomplished through physical contact.

Extremophiles: People who love to play on the edge.

Go get a cookie: This phrase means, "If you don't like the scene you're watching, leave that area." By inference, it means, "Don't say something negative or questioning about someone's scene unless you are recognized as a Dungeon Monitor" at that party.

Gor: Short for *Gorean*—a subculture that grew out of the science fiction novels of John Norman, based on a belief that in the natural order, all males are inherently dominant over all females. There are communities of people who live according to Gorean customs, much as there are communities of people who live according to some other aspect of BDSM customs.

(NOTE: The **Gorean** philosophy of a male-dominated Master/slave world sprung from John Norman's science fiction novels. Even though many of the *visible* protocols seem almost identical, there are substantial differences between the way Master/slave relationships are enacted in the gay male leather culture, the leather dyke community, the heterosexual leather culture, the general BDSM culture, and in the Gorean culture.)

Hotdogging: Playing dangerously, stupidly, unsafely, or showing off. This is most often seen when a new and inexperienced Top wants to impress their bottom (or the people at a play party who are watching). Tops who are hotdogging are not paying attention to their bottom, they are egocentrically soaking up the audience's reaction to the scene. (See: Now watch this.)

Hurt versus harm: For the sake of this book, *hurt* is "ouch" but *harm* can last a lifetime. Thus, the sentence, "I will be glad to hurt you if you'd like, but I definitely do not wish to harm you" makes sense. In your mind, you can substitute the phrase *intense sensations* for "hurt."

Invisible collar: Phrase that describes the lingering emotional connection between people after an emotionally bonding experience that does not end decisively. (Coined by M. Jen Fairfield in about 2014.)

Kinky: Slang for people *who enjoy adventuresome sex* which is, itself, a euphemism for BDSM. (Note: Some BDSM relationships can be mostly about discipline and non-sexual aspects of domination and service submission. This distinguishes such relationships from those in the vanilla world.)

Kinsey scale: The 0-6 Kinsey scale (also called the Heterosexual-Homosexual Rating Scale) attempts to describe a person's sexual orientation. In this scale, zero means that the person is exclusively heterosexual and six means that the person is exclusively homosexual.

Leather, Leathermen, Leathersex: The leather subculture is one of many facets of semi-organized alternative sexuality. The term originally described man-to-man S/M relationships and sexual activity. In recent decades, the leather community has almost come to be viewed as a subset of BDSM culture rather than a descendant of a larger gay culture. Almost anything that is said about leather and its evolution to present times is subject to challenge.

At the risk of oversimplification, four essential elements of leather are:

- Leather attire: A *physical symbol of a belief system.*
  - What we wear tells everyone what we are.
  - Pins on our leather vests tell everyone where we've been.
- It is the outward manifestation of subculture that holds certain common beliefs.
  - Honor
  - Integrity
  - Loyalty
  - Trust
- Leather sexuality: Leathersex is about the mind, about an exchange of power, *about using the senses.*
  - the feel of restraints—whether physical or mental

- ⊙ the smell of the body
- ⊙ the taste of another's skin
- ⊙ the sound of a flogger
- ⊙ the look of the remaining marks and bruises

○ Leather community: We socialize with other leather people, in groups, clubs, and at play parties. This includes our leather community, our leather family, and –more generally – our network of leather friends.

○ Leather spirit is by far the broadest trait. This means **living the values; walking the walk.** This transcends attire, sexuality, and community to allow us to become a part of a larger whole. Finally, we have a place where we belong.

Little: A person of either gender who enjoys speaking/acting/dressing as though they are 4, 7, 10, etc. They are likely to have stuffed animals on their beds and enjoy coloring with pencils and crayons. While a "little" may enjoy "little boy" or "little girl" activities, they are very different from age players who are in the headspace of someone who is 4, 7, 10, etc.

Limits: Boundaries negotiated between the Top and bottom before a scene. Hard limits represent "do not do these" topics; soft limits represent "I'd rather you not do these" topics.

Masochism: In psychiatry, the condition in which sexual gratification depends on suffering physical pain or humiliation; gratification gained from pain, deprivation, degradation, etc., inflicted or imposed on oneself, either as a result of one's own actions or the actions of others, especially the tendency to seek this form of gratification.

Master and slave: Usually applied to a 24/7 relationship structure wherein the subordinate person (slave) has surrendered authority over themselves and pledged to serve and obey their Master who now exerts total control (and offers total protection) for the subordinate.

Munch: Munches are intended to be non-threatening social gatherings to help those who are curious about BDSM meet others who may be able to help them become more comfortable and better informed.

Munches can also be a place to get advice about BDSM experiences, make friends, and perhaps flirt a little.

Negotiating/negotiations: The process of determining what will and will not go on in a play scene—or in a relationship. As some people consider the scene to start with negotiations, this is not a time to be interrupted.

Neuro-Linguistic Programming (NLP): Neuro-Linguistic Programming is like a user's manual for the brain. Taking an NLP training is like learning how to become fluent in the language of your mind so that the ever-so-helpful "server" that is your unconscious will finally understand what you actually want out of life. NLP is the study of excellent communication—both with yourself and with others. It is an attitude and a methodology of knowing how to achieve your goals and get results.

"Now watch this!" According to expert BDSM witness Jay Wiseman, JD, there is a 100% correlation between a Top saying, "Now watch this!" and a scene going bad.

Old Guard: A term used to describe a near-mythical time in gay leather history when returned GIs from World War II blended some features of their military experiences with their kinky interests to produce a subculture that over time became known as *leather*. Some of the distant echoes of their quasi-military rules of protocol, inclusion, and exclusion can still be seen in today's BDSM society.

Pansexual: A pansexual is someone who can be attracted to males, females, transgender people, and those who identify as non-binary (not female or male).

Pavlovian response: Psychologist Ivan Pavlov developed the concept of behavioral conditioning. In his classic experiment, he trained a dog to salivate at the sound of a bell by conditioning the dog to associate the sound of the bell with being fed. More currently, hypnotists create conditioned responses by *anchoring* them in your subconscious.

Pick-up Scenes: A "pick-up" scene is one that happens spontaneously at a play party. You hadn't negotiated play with this person before the party. It's a pleasant surprise.

Play: The term used by those in the BDSM community for an SM scene involving a Top (doing the action) and a bottom (receiving the action). (See also, "work.")

Protocols and such:

- **Protocols** are a written statement of how things are to be done. In a D/s or M/s relationship, a protocol explains how the D-type wants the s-type to do things. This can range from sorting the mail to setting the table or keeping the closet clean.

- **Rituals** are a collection of protocols the D-type has designed to create a specific state of mind for the s-type, particularly about their roles. Rituals may concern how the D-type and s-type interact in a certain setting (such as starting or ending a scene). Rituals may also be created to celebrate some of the mechanics of time spent together (greeting rituals, bathing rituals, dining rituals).

- **Ceremonies** combine a number of rituals into a larger event that has a specific start and stop time. Ceremonies also have established formats. You would never confuse a wedding ceremony for a Thanksgiving Day ceremony, etc.

RACK (Risk Aware Consensual Kink): A standard of SM play often used by established couples. Here, the Top knows how to read the bottom's reactions and also has the authority to judge when to continue or end a scene based on their knowledge of that bottom. The bottom trusts their Top to manage / control the scene without input. RACK-level play assumes the Top will not intentionally harm the bottom.

Sadism: In psychiatry, the condition in which sexual gratification is linked with causing pain or degradation to others. (See also, masochism, sensationist.)

SAM (Smart-Assed Masochist): The name sometimes associated with a bottom who tries to direct the Top's play during a scene. If you hear something like, "Sheesh! You hit like my sister! Who taught you to throw that flogger?" you've got a SAM on your hands.

SM: Sadomasochism. The psychological tendency or sexual practice characterized by both sadism and masochism.

SM play/scenes: Activities between two or more people of any gender that involve giving and receiving intense sensations such as spanking, flogging, whipping, etc. for their mutual and consensual enjoyment.

SM techniques: Methods such as spanking, whipping, bondage, or electro-stimulation that sadists may use to cause masochists to feel the desired sensations.

SSC (Safe, Sane, and Consensual): A slogan (coined by slave david stein) used to summarize the minimal physical/psychological conditions most people consider acceptable for SM play to take place. Those using SSC play standards use "colors" to signal their ongoing consent during a scene. (See: "Colors," above.)

Safe-call: A procedure used when meeting someone for the first time (or even when meeting someone that you don't know well) that ensures that someone else knows what you're doing, who you are meeting with, where you'll be meeting, and that you are safe.

Safewords: Words that you and your partner have agreed to use to stop the play entirely (such as, *red*), or to slow it down a bit (such as, *yellow*). One uses words such as *red* because words such as, "No" or "stop" or "Ouch, no, stop!" may be part of the scene. (See "Colors," above.)

Scene going bad / Scene went bad: A slang expression describing a scene where an accident happened or appears about to happen. This phrase can also be used when the bottom has an unexpected emotional reaction to something ("hits a landmine") or the Top is inept.

Sensationist: A *sensationist* enjoys the wide-ranging sensations available from SM play but may not be a masochist—someone who derives erotic stimulation from pain. (See also: sadist, masochist.)

Service Top: Someone whose pleasure comes from giving SM pleasure to others without getting sexual arousal from the acts. That is, the Top is not a sadist, but is enjoying providing intense sensations to another, often being directed or limited by the bottom. A service Top's intent is to fulfill the wishes and desires of the person bottoming for them. Even though a service Top may not dominate the scene in terms of a D/s dynamic, they do control the scene. As the phrase implies, the Top is doing something for the sake of the bottom.

Sex-role stereotyping: The general public stereotype is that Doms are men with sadistic/Top preferences and that submissives are women who have masochistic/bottom preferences. These are stereotypes and are far from the way roles are practiced within this culture. In reality, Dominants can be male or female, masochists or sadists, and of any sexual orientation. So can submissives.

Spanko: Someone who has eroticized spanking; someone who gets erotic pleasure either from spanking someone or from being spanked (or both). Unlike spankings in the BDSM community, a spanko scene is often filled with banter between the Top and bottom and (possibly) with those standing around and watching. Spanko events often involve bratty bottoms who will readily go up to an available Top (identified by the color of their nametag) and bait them into chasing after them and scolding them for being such a bad girl/boy, thus starting the scene.

Submissive **versus** *slave:* Once again, we caution readers that the characteristics listed under *submissive* and *slave* are generalizations based on our decades-long research and experiences living within (and studying) the field of BDSM and Master/slave relations. These descriptions are certainly not intended to be taken as *rules.* These are our distinctions and may not be generally accepted by others practicing D/s or M/s structures. As you grow in BDSM experience, what we write in this book generally—and the following points about distinctions between *submissive* and *slave* specifically—may make more sense to you.

We'll begin by proposing that *submissive* and *slave* motivations and behaviors aren't quite the same. While one is certainly not better than the other, one set of behaviors is more likely to fit some people than others.

submissive

○ D/s relationships are based on power *exchange* (meaning that the submissive who normally has personal authority over what they, themselves, may or may not do or have done to them can give or exchange that power to the Dom/me for a prescribed period).

- submissives have a strong desire to serve—but under certain negotiated conditions.

- Typically, the negotiated areas include the submissive's term of service, the length of that service, the hard and soft limits, and the safewords.

- The submissive will also negotiate those aspects of their life that the Dom doesn't control. These aspects often include the submissive's biological family and children, work, education, and religious observance.

- The conditions under which the submissive is willing to serve can be renegotiated. (This is a major issue: The submissive retains the personal authority to ask their Dominant to renegotiate their terms of service, but the Dominant is under no obligation to accept the newly proposed conditions.)

- If the Dom breaks the submissive's hard limits, the scene would end and—in the case of a breach of a relationship trust—the relationship could end.

- The Dom may be permitted to break *soft limits* (things the submissive has said they really aren't interested in) after discussing it with the submissive and obtaining their permission.

- In most cases, submissives cross back and forth between retaining and surrendering control over some aspect of their lives and continue to make decisions in the areas that are off-limits for their Dom.

- A submissive re-submits to the Dom at the start of any scene or activity over which the Dom has negotiated authority. Importantly, the submissive retains the choice as to whether or not to submit to the Dom.

slave, consensual

- M/s relationship is based on authority transfer. This means that once the person who is to become the slave has, in fact, surrendered personal authority over him/herself to their

Master/Owner, they no longer have the personal power to make decisions for him/herself. Thus, a slave would not have the authority to enter into a D/s scene with someone other than their Master/Owner without that Master/Owner's specifically transferring THEIR authority over their own slave to another person.

O At least in theory, the slave gives up all rights to make personal decisions and becomes the property of a Master or Owner.

O The core values are *service* and *obedience*.

O The slave gives up the right to say "No" to his or her Master. In its place, a slave may say, "Sir, if it pleases you, Sir" (to mean, "Master, I really would rather not do that.") or "Sir, only if it pleases you, Sir," which is as close to "No" as a slave is permitted. (Note: The Master has an ethical obligation to push through an "only if" reply only so long as the Master thinks that doing so remains in the slave's best interest. Requiring a slave to proceed through an "only if" command on the Master's whim violates the basic Master/slave pact on the Master's part and represents an ethical violation.)

O As a slave cannot *red out*, a slave has developed deep trust and accepted their Master's limits and does what is asked of them regardless of their feelings about it. ("What does *liking it* have to do with it?")

O In many cases, a slave will give up their rights to personal property and will continue to work for the benefit of their Master's household or business.

O A slave's purpose is to make the Master's life easier. In that regard, a slave is expected to know their Master's wants and likes to the extent that the slave can take independent action on the Master's behalf (proactive rather than reactive; to show initiative as a thinking person),

O If a slave removes their own collar, it constitutes withdrawal from the relationship,

O A slave may be more interested in taking care of others (service heart) than in being taken care of (*sorts by others* in psychology-speak)

- A slave may very well be a dominant in most other aspects of their life, but they have chosen to be submissive to (or simply to serve) one single person,

Subordinate **versus** *submissive* **versus** *slave*: A person who is normally dominant who has chosen to serve another Dominant. Think of the relationship between a Captain and a Colonel or a Chief Operating Officer to their Chief Executive Officer. The Captain and the COO are not submissives, they are subordinate officers. In the world of Masters and slaves, it is more correct to refer to the slave as a subordinate unless they have a submissive personality.

Subspace: Similar to *runner's high*, this is an altered state of mind/body dissociation, detached from worldly cares, that is often obtained by bottoms during an SM play scene. (See also: Top-space.)

Switch—common use: Someone who enjoys being either the Top or the bottom; enjoys giving or receiving physical SM stimulation. Among Leathermen, switches are sometimes referred to as *versatile*.

Switch—less common use: Someone who is willing to take either the leadership or subordinate role in a relationship depending upon the *chemistry* or *connection* with a particular partner. When used this way, a person is referred to as a **psychological switch**. While *physical switches* can easily switch within their relationship, psychological switches do not. Psychological switches would have relationships wherein their roles are different—dominant in one relationship and subordinate (not necessarily submissive) in the other. This is an advanced and controversial topic, and we only touch on it in this book.)

Top: The person *doing* the action.

Top/bottom play: Sensation play with SM toys/tools—no psychological dynamic, no power exchange. *Top* and *bottom* are terms that relate to physical action only. The Top spanks the bottom. The Top or the bottom may be a dominant person or a submissive person of either gender. The terms *Top* and *bottom* only describe *roles* while *dominant* and *submissive* describe how people interact in relationships. The decision to Top or bottom is only a decision of which person wishes to receive or inflict sensations that the tools/toys produce when handled by someone who has been properly trained.

Top-space: A state of intense focus and concentration defined as expert skill/knowledge being carried out under optimal conditions. In psychology, this condition is referred to as being "in the zone." This concept was developed by psychologist Mihaly Csikszentmihalyi and published in *Flow: The Psychology of Optimal Experience* (New York, Harper and Row Book Club Edition, 1990. Print.). In BDSM, this state is sometimes attained by a Top during particularly intense scenes. You mostly know you've been in it when you try to come out of it.

Top-drop and sub-drop: The letdown that can occur after your body has been flooded with adrenaline and/or dopamine.

Toys/tools: The implements or equipment used in a BDSM scene. The gay men's leather community historically referred to this equipment as *tools* while the BDSM community uses the term *toys*. Obviously, the mindset of someone "working with the bottom" is very different than that of someone "playing with the bottom." (See also: "play" and "work.")

Tyranny of technique: The *tyranny of technique* is a phrase created by Guy Baldwin in about 2005 to describe kinksters who seem to be focused on getting the mechanics of play correct at the cost of the connection they are trying to establish with their bottom.

Vanilla: The term used by those in the BDSM community for those who are not. It's not a pejorative term, simply a descriptor. Typical uses: vanilla sex, land of vanillas, etc.

Work: The term used by those in the Leather community for an SM scene involving a Top (doing the action) and a bottom (receiving the action). (See also: "play.")

"WYSIWYG" or "not WYSIWYG": This term comes from the world of IT and means, "What You See Is What You Get." My typical use: "Unlike the WYSIWYG Vanilla World where what you see is what you get, the BDSM world is full of paradoxes and actions whose meanings may not be immediately obvious."

About the Authors

Robert J. Rubel, Ph.D.

Robert Rubel (Dr. Bob), author, educator, and photographer, is an educational sociologist and researcher by training. He currently has over a dozen books in print and two DVDs. Four of his books are on Master/slave topics, two are on advanced sex techniques, one is on fire play, and three are erotic art photo books. His DVDs include fire play and beginning impact play.

Recipient of the 2008 Pantheon of Leather's Community Choice Award (man), Dr. Bob has been involved in the BDSM and Total Power Exchange (TPE) scene since the summer of 2001, throwing himself into the literature of the field as though it were an academic study. He presents, judges, and sells his books at weekend kink conferences throughout the year.

The Goddess Indigo

The Goddess Indigo never thought of herself as a "dominant" person; people simply did what she asked them to do. This pattern began when she transformed her first boyfriend into "house-slave" decades before discovering the term "BDSM" online. That initial "authority-transfer," coupled with her voracious appetite for knowledge, launched her spiritual odyssey into the world of Masters and slaves (M/s).

The Goddess (an international educator with a unique brand of irreverent humor) has wide-ranging experiences. She ran the largest gathering of human equines in the U.S. (*Camp Crucible* in Maryland), yet thrives on emceeing events. She co-directs MAsT Austin (Masters And slaves Together); founded a female-led dynamics group (MAsT Austin—DOMINA); and chairs Austin's *Authority-Imbalanced Dynamics* monthly discussion munch. Previously, she has hosted *The Leather Line* radio show (KPFT, FM 90.1 in Houston), and participated in performance art for Art Erotica and for *International Ms Leather* (IMsL).

The Goddess is Matriarch of the Leather Family *Genus Indigo,* and owns Dr. Bob, her slave and force-multiplier. She humbly appreciates the continued requests to teach about her own personal passion, sustainable female-led dynamics.

Books by the Authors

All listed (and future) books can be purchased through Amazon or through our website, GoddessAndDoc.com

BOOKS BY DR. BOB AND THE GODDESS INDIGO

In One Ear and Out the Other: Guide for effective communication

Do you listen to respond or listen to understand? While many books are written about how to get your point across, effective communication is about transmitting and receiving messages as close to the intended meaning as possible. What caused the deterioration of the intended meaning? You.

Communication is like a two-way street filled with loud and distracting traffic, barriers, and blockades. Imagine that you are on one side of that street, and the person trying to speak with you is on the other side. Neither of you can cross, and you are trying to get messages back-and-forth.

In reality, that street noise represents the many barriers created by your personal perspectives and filters that you have been accumulating your entire life. Unfortunately, they often interfere with your ability to clearly understand or clearly transmit a message.

So… How do we get from this noisy, busy street to better understanding?

The first step in truly listening is learning how to get out of your own way. The roadmap to becoming an effective communicator lies within.

ROBERT J. RUBEL AND M. JEN FAIRFIELD

BDSM Mastery—Basics: Your guide to play, parties, and scene protocols.

This is not a book that explains what BDSM *is*, this is a book that explains what BDSM *is all about*. This is a book that enables someone with zero BDSM experience to walk confidently into their first munch or club meeting. This is also a book for people who have been involved in the community for a while and are now interested in understanding how the puzzle pieces fit together. Once you've finished this book, you'll have as much BDSM knowledge as someone who has been actively in the public scene for about five years.

BDSM Mastery—Relationships: A guide for creating mindful relationships for Dominants and submissives

This is a book about relationships. Adventuresome relationships. Relationships that are not exactly like *vanilla* relationships (traditional relationships as practiced by the average couple you'd meet at a baseball game). BDSM relationships differ from vanilla relationships in two specific ways:

- ⦿ First, they involve a power-imbalanced structure (one person is clearly in charge, and the other person is clearly following);

- ⦿ Second, the kind of sex that adventuresome folk practice is, well, *not vanilla*.

This book speaks to those who are starting out in BDSM, or are involved with someone in a BDSM-based relationship. Reading this book will save each of you a lot of heartache, frustration, and anger.

Master/slave Mastery: Updated handbook of concepts, approaches, and practices (2014)

> This is the first book in a series devoted to Master/slave mastery. It is intended to help people start their relationship thoughtfully. It discusses cautions about potential Masters and potential slaves.

> We distinguish between D/s and M/s relationships. D/s is more about power exchange while M/s is more about authority-transfer. D/s is more about where you fall on the scale of dominance and submission; M/s is about the roles you each play.

> Because of these differences, we believe that D/s and M/s have different "rules of engagement." This book helps explain some of those "rules," as we've come to understand them.

> This book is intended to provide important tips and tools for building a firm relationship.

Master/slave Mastery—Advanced: Refining the fire—ideas that matter

> This book assumes that readers have substantial 24/7 M/s experience.

> This is an advanced Master/slave book. It is for people with very strong core values who have been doing M/s for 5+ years (or been heavily involved in D/s for that long). This is for people who know a lot about a lot and are open to thinking about what they know in a different way. It is a "content-heavy" book. You'll want about five years of experience to be able to read it comfortably. Readers should thoroughly understand the difference between a D/s culture and an M/s culture.

> This book presents many viewpoints on M/s relationships. I've been attending M/s conferences since 2003 and have taken good notes. Those notes, my 13 years living 24/7 M/s, and extensive discussions with hundreds of people who identify with Mastery and slavery have been combined to create this book. Jen and I explain how strong leaders can combine with strong, supportive followers to make a magical relationship.

Unlike the fictional world of Masters and slaves, this book discusses the very real challenges and opportunities available to long-term M/s couples.

Master/slave Mastery—Protocols: Focusing the intent of your relationship (Fairfield is lead author)

This book is a map to help others design their own personal protocols. It provides countless tips and techniques for Masters so they can clarify how they, themselves want to be served. The book gives details about how we (within our relationship) translated those wishes into elegant service.

In our experience, a protocol manual is much more than documenting rules of service. Writing a protocol manual helps you examine and refine your relationship and your relationship management style. The very process of creating a manual such as this reveals the kinds of service a Master *really* wants from the slave and the kinds of service the slave can actually deliver. In that light, writing a protocol manual is an exercise in clarifying the intent of your relationship.

Is THAT what they meant? A book of practical communication insights

Many of our adult behaviors are largely invisible to us because they're accepted and supported by our culture. It doesn't occur to us to question our own (or our partner's) basic assumptions about who we are and how we interact in the world. It's difficult to step aside from yourself and explore *why* you think as you do. The more you understand how you (and those with whom you're speaking) take in information, the easier the communication becomes. This book is intended to help you decipher what others are saying and also to help you realize why some of your messages are not being heard the way you intended them.

OTHER BOOKS OR DVDS BY ROBERT J. RUBEL

○ *Flames of Passion: Handbook of Erotic Fire Play* (With David Walker) Las Vegas: Nazca Plains, 2006.

○ *Fire Play: A Safety Training Course* (70-minute DVD plus 48-page book) Las Vegas: Nazca Plains, 2012

○ *Impact Play 101: Building Your Skills* (70-minute DVD plus 48-page book) Las Vegas: Nazca Plains, 2012

○ *Squirms, Screams, and Squirts: Handbook for going from great sex to extraordinary sex* Las Vegas: Nazca Plains, 2008

○ *Squirms, Screams, and Squirts: The Workbook* Las Vegas: Nazca Plains, 2009

○ *Screams of Pleasure: Guide for Extraordinary Sex for those with Erectile Dysfunction* (Slightly revised version of Squirms, Screams, and Squirts) Las Vegas: Nazca Plains, 2009

Books of Erotic and Fetish Art: Three books on erotic and fetish photography titled (with an eye towards perverse humor) were published by the Nazca Plains Corp (Las Vegas) 2006.

○ *Parts: The Erotic Photographic Art of Robert J. Rubel, PhD.*

○ *Wholes: The Erotic Photographic Art of Robert J. Rubel, PhD.*

○ *Holes: The Erotic Photographic Art of Robert J. Rubel, PhD.*

Edited Publications: Bob served as the Managing Editor of *Power Exchange Magazine* in 2007-2008. Issue themes included:

○ *Master/slave Relations—male Master*

○ *Master/slave Relations—female Master*

○ *Bootblacking*

○ *FemDomme*

○ *Pony Play*

○ *Polyamory*

○ *Daddy/boy*

○ *Leather Spirituality*

○ *Pup/Trainer*

In 2007 Bob made a marketing decision and transformed *Power Exchange Magazine* into a small book format. This series, *Power Exchange Books' Resource Series,* are 100-page books on focused topics of interest to BDSM or Leather folk. The series is about the "why" of what we do, not the "how." Dr. Bob served as the Series editor, but each collection of essays was managed by someone with knowledge in that specific field.

Power Exchange Books' *Resource Series*

- *Playing with Disabilities*
- *The Art of Slavery*
- *Protocols: A Variety of Views*
- *Rope, Bondage, and Power*
- *Age Play*

www.ingramcontent.com/pod-product-compliance
Lightning Source LLC
Chambersburg PA
CBHW022022090426
42739CB00006BA/246